Battle Orders • 14

Japanese Army in World War II

The South Pacific and New Guinea, 1942–43

Gordon L Rottman
Series editors Marcus Cowper and Nikolai Bogdanovic

First published in Great Britain in 2005 by Osprey Publishing,
Midland House, West Way, Botley, Oxford OX2 0PH, United Kingdom
443 Park Avenue South, New York, NY 10016, USA
Email: info@ospreypublishing.com

ISBN 1 84176 870 7

Design: Bounford.com, Royston, UK
Maps by Bounford.com, Royston, UK
Index by Alan Thatcher
Originated by The Electronic Page Company, Cwmbran, UK
Printed and bound in China through Bookbuilders

05 06 07 08 09 10 9 8 7 6 5 4 3 2 1

A CIP catalog record for this book is available from the British Library.

For a catalog of all books published by Osprey Military and Aviation please contact:
NORTH AMERICA
Osprey Direct, 2427 Bond Street, University Park, IL 60466, USA
E-mail: info@ospreydirectusa.com

ALL OTHER REGIONS
Osprey Direct UK, P.O. Box 140, Wellingborough, Northants, NN8 2FA, UK
E-mail: info@ospreydirect.co.uk

www.ospreypublishing.com

Image credits

Unless otherwise indicated, the photographic images that appear
in this work are from the US National Archives.

Author's note

In the tree diagrams and maps in this volume, Japanese units and
movements are depicted in red, with enemy (Allied) units in black,
as per Japanese practice. For a key to the symbols used in this
volume, see below.
Unit designations: Japanese battalions organic to infantry and
artillery regiments are designated with the battalion Roman
number followed by the regimental Arabic number; for example,
I/7 or II/10. Companies and batteries organic to infantry and
artillery regiments are designated with the company/battery
Arabic number; for example, "1/I/2 Infantry" stands for "1st
Company, I Battalion, 2d Infantry Regiment." Companies organic
to cavalry, reconnaissance, engineer, and transport regiments,
which did not have internal battalions, are designated by Arabic
company and Arabic regimental numbers; for example, "2/12
Engineer" refers to "2d Company, 12th Engineer Regiment."
Japanese personal names are shown according to Japanese
custom, with the family name first and the given name last.
Contemporary place names are used in this book.

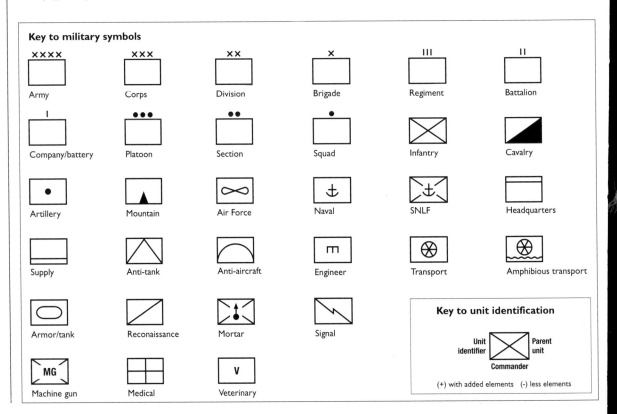

Contents

Introduction

Japan's successful conquest of the South Pacific and Southwest Asia from December 8, 1941 through to June 1942 saw few setbacks. The commencement of the Pacific War (*Taiheiyo Senso*), coupled with the China Incident (*Shina Jihen*) on-going since 1931, was what Japan called the Greater Southeast Asia War (*Dai Toa Senso Senkum*)—more commonly known as World War II. The Southern Operations that began the Pacific War comprised a complex series of widely scattered operations aimed at neutralizing American, Commonwealth, and Dutch forces, seizing regions rich in economic resources, and securing an outer defense line for the "Greater Southeast Asia Co-prosperity Sphere" (*Dai Toa Kyoei-Ken*).

The American bastion of the Philippines, the Netherlands East Indies (NEI), and Commonwealth possessions of the Gilbert, Bismarck, and Solomon islands were occupied, and troops were landed on Eastern New Guinea. Commonwealth forces were driven from Malaya, Thailand and most of Burma, and Hong Kong and Singapore were taken by the Japanese. All of the objectives were secured with light to moderate losses well within the projected timeframe, with the notable exception of the Philippines. Rather than securing the vast archipelago within the allotted 50 days, it required five months. In addition, the occupation resulted in heavy losses and required reinforcements to be sent in.

The Southern Operation, or Z Operation, was conducted by the Southern Army under the command of Gen Count Terauchi Hisaichi (also listed as Juichi) headquartered in Saigon, French Indochina. Under his command were four armies, 11 divisions, and six brigade equivalents plus substantial support, service, and air units. Additional units were deployed during the course of the Southern Operation.

At the beginning of the war the Imperial Japanese Army (*Dai Nippon Teikoku Rikugun*, or simply *Kogun*, herafter abbreviated to IJA) consisted of 51 divisions and 59 brigade equivalents. Surprisingly only nine new divisions had been organized in 1940 and one in 1941, with most intended for China rather than in preparation for facing the Allied counteroffensive. Numerous brigade equivalents, service, and air units had been raised though, as were independent mixed brigades (IMBs) and garrison units to secure occupied territories. Only seven infantry divisions were activated in the spring of 1942.

With the Philippines, Malaya, NEI, Bismarcks, and the Solomons secured, the Imperial Japanese Navy (IJN) planned further conquests, having longer-ranged goals than the IJA. Rabaul on New Britain would be a base from which to continue the conquest. The IJA thought of Rabaul only as an out-guard for the naval base at Truk in the Carolines. The IJN, in cooperation with the IJA, desired to seize Port Moresby on the south coast of Papua in May; Midway and the western Aleutian Islands in June, hoping for a decisive engagement with the US Pacific Fleet; New Caledonia in July; and Fiji and Samoa in August. The goal was to break the Southern Lifeline between America and Australia. Future plans were even more ambitious, with proposals to invade Hawaii, northern Australia, and Ceylon.

The first book in this series, Battle Orders 9: *Japanese Army in World War II: Conquest of the Pacific 1941–42*, covers the period from the beginning of the Greater East Asia War in December 1941 to the war's turning point in June 1942, the Battle of Midway. Future proposed volumes in this series will cover the 1944–45 defense of the Philippines and Central and West Pacific operations in 1943–45.

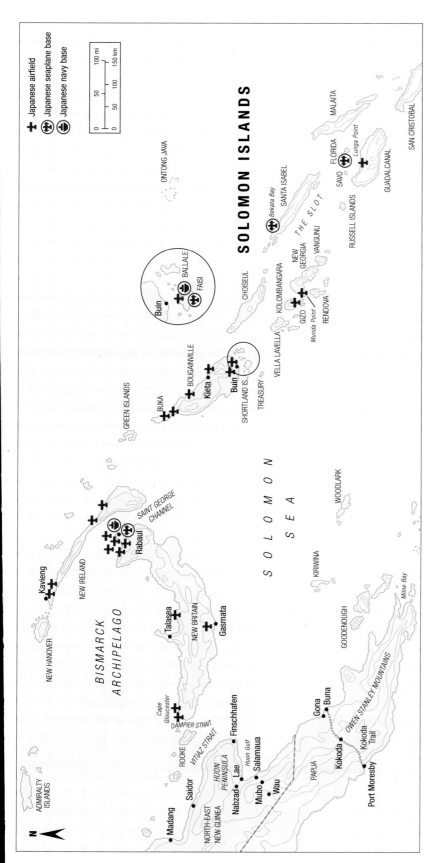

The Southeastern Area was under the operational control of the IJN. Following the US invasion of Guadalcanal, the IJA's presence in the area vastly increased. The Japanese airfields, and seaplane and naval bases are shown on this map.

5

Combat mission

While the IJN still anticipated the decisive engagement with the US Pacific Fleet and further expansion to secure the conquered regions, the Imperial General Headquarters (IGHQ, *Daikairei Dai*) prepared for the Western powers' counteroffensive. A National Defense Zone would be established in Burma and down through the NEI, western New Guinea, the Caroline and Marshall Islands (Japanese Mandated Territory), with an anchor point on remote Wake Island in the north. Eastern New Guinea, outside the Zone, would be secured, as would the Gilberts, Bismarcks, and Solomons to serve as buffer zones.

1942–43 expansion

The war saw only a modest expansion of the infantry force with the activation of the 58th, 59th, 60th, 68th, 69th, 70th, and 71st divisions during 1942. These were lightly equipped security divisions raised in China, with the exception of the 71st, a standard B infantry division organized in Manchuria. The security divisions were organized from the 18th, 10th, 11th, 14th, 16th, and 20th IMBs, respectively. The 71st Division's cadre was provided by the 140th Infantry Regiment and Hunchan Garrison Unit. These divisions lacked artillery and reconnaissance units, and possessed eight infantry battalions and only minimal engineer and service units. Only one new independent mixed brigade, 1st IMB, was raised in 1942 in Japan. By the end of 1942, Japan fielded 58 infantry divisions and 54 brigade equivalents as opposed to the 51 divisions and 59 brigade equivalents it possessed in December 1941. Three modest tank divisions were also raised in 1942. Since most of the IMBs absorbed into the new divisions had five independent infantry battalions (IIBs), and coupled with replacing combat losses, there was little increase in combat strength. It was more of a reallocation of manpower.

Even with combat losses the IJA experienced little difficulty equipping the new units. The security divisions lacked artillery and were allotted fewer heavy infantry weapons than infantry divisions. While they did possess significant numbers of 7.5cm regimental guns, they had no 7cm battalion guns. Stocks of 7.5cm regimental guns were adequate as it had once been the standard mountain gun, but was relegated to its new role when replaced in 1934 and large numbers were on-hand. The 71st Division received a mountain artillery regiment. Only 130 artillery pieces over 10.5cm were produced in 1942, 250 10cm weapons (actually 10.5cm), and 2,130 smaller caliber pieces (7.5cm and below). Motor transport and engineer equipment were also in short supply and production would continue to drop. Tank production was 634 lights and 531 mediums, with 26 self-propelled guns. Light tank production was intentionally reduced at the end of 1942 with only a slight increase in medium tank production. There was a major increase in tankette production through 1942, which totalled 442, compared to 88 in 1941.

Even after the Allies shifted to the offensive in late 1942, Japan organized only 12 more temporary infantry divisions in 1943: 30th in Korea; 1st Guards, 42d, 43d, 46th, 47th and 61st in Japan; and 31st, 62d,

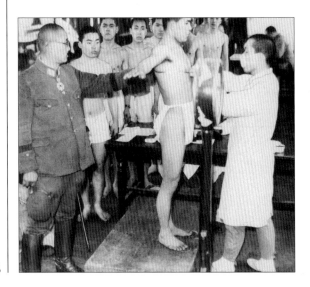

The Imperial Japanese Army had expanded greatly well before the outbreak of the Pacific War, in response to the China Incident. Recruiting standards were maintained through to 1942, but were then lowered to provide manpower for new units and to replace combat losses.

The IJA was still very much equipped as per an army of the 1930s. It relied extensively on horse transport, which in China had not proved to be a liability. Here a 7.5cm Type 41 (1908) infantry gun unit enters Tientsin, China.

63d, 64th and 65th in China. The 30th and 31st were organized from regiments reassigned from six triangularized square divisions to become standard B divisions themselves. The 42d, 43d, 46th, 47th, and 61st divisions absorbed the 62d, 63d, 66th, 67th, and 61st three-regiment Independent Infantry Groups respectively, as standard B divisions. The 62d, 63d, 64th, and 65th divisions were converted from the 4th, 15th, 12th, and 13th IMBs respectively, as security divisions. Those raised in Japan were mainly sent to garrison occupied territories, but two went to China. Eleven IMBs were raised in 1943: the 23d, and the 25th–34th. Most absorbed existing independent garrison units, field replacement units, and drafts from various divisions. They mainly garrisoned the NEI and the Philippines. The 1st–4th Amphibious Brigades were also organized in 1943 with the mission of defending islands. These will be discussed in the forthcoming Battle Orders title on the Japanese Army in the Central and West Pacific, 1943–45 along with sea operations divisions.

The production of equipment and some categories of armament fell in 1943. The IJA received fewer trucks than it had lost in action, or had sunk on ships, or had become worn out. Only 1,540 7.5cm and smaller-caliber artillery pieces were produced, 110 10cm pieces, and 90 15cm or larger-caliber pieces. Infantry guns and antitank guns were in short supply. Mortar production did increase. Medium tank production had increased slightly to 554, but only 232 lights and 14 self-propelled guns were built. Tank production would be slashed even more drastically by the end of 1943 though, but the numbers of tankettes, having proved themselves well-suited to security duty in China, would increase, with 615 built. There was little need for tanks in the Pacific and steel production was needed for ships and other weapons. Limited tank development continued though.

Parachute-retarded fragmentation bombs being dropped on one of Rabaul's five airfields. The neutralization of Rabaul on New Britain was a main Allied goal throughout 1942 and 1943. The Japanese made every effort to retain the base, but its aircraft and shipping were destroyed, and it was cut off from external support. The Allies by-passed the base, and it could do little but hold out until the war's end.

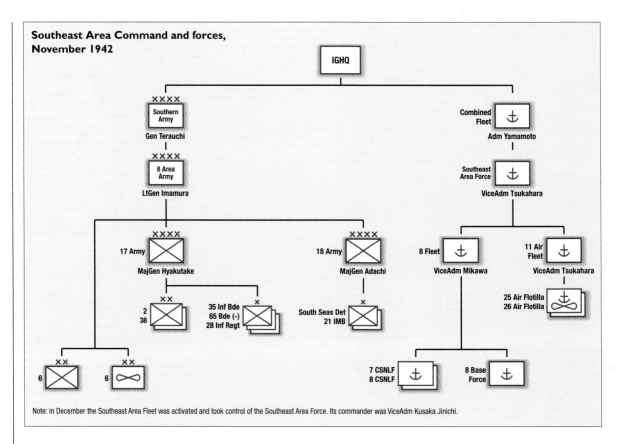

Southeast Area Command and forces, November 1942

IGHQ

Southern Army — Gen Terauchi (XXXX)

8 Area Army — LtGen Imamura (XXXX)

17 Army — MajGen Hyakutake (XXXX)

2
38 (XX)

35 Inf Bde
65 Bde (-)
28 Inf Regt (x)

6 (XX)

6 (XX)

18 Army — MajGen Adachi (XXXX)

South Seas Det
21 IMB (x)

Combined Fleet — Adm Yamamoto

Southeast Area Force — ViceAdm Tsukahara

8 Fleet — ViceAdm Mikawa

11 Air Fleet — ViceAdm Tsukahara

25 Air Flotilla
26 Air Flotilla

7 CSNLF
8 CSNLF

8 Base Force

Note: in December the Southeast Area Fleet was activated and took control of the Southeast Area Force. Its commander was ViceAdm Kusaka Jinichi.

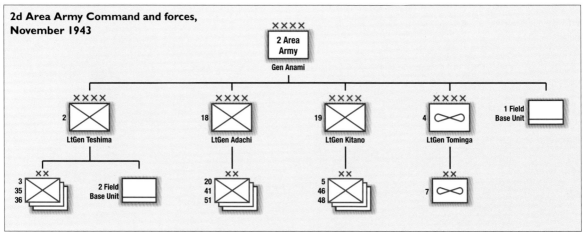

2d Area Army Command and forces, November 1943

2 Area Army — Gen Anami (XXXX)

2 — LtGen Teshima (XXXX)

3
35
36 (XX)

2 Field Base Unit

18 — LtGen Adachi (XXXX)

20
41
51 (XX)

19 — LtGen Kitano (XXXX)

5
46
48 (XX)

4 — LtGen Tominga (XXXX)

7 (XX)

1 Field Base Unit

Plans for the Solomons and New Guinea

With the Bismarck Archipelago (New Britain, New Ireland, and the Admiralty Islands) successfully occupied between late January and early April 1942, the IJA and IJN prepared to conduct further operations to the south. Rabaul on New Britain would be developed as a major naval and air base to protect the southern approaches to the Mandates and from which to launch further operations to the south and southeast. To provide out-guards for Rabaul, Tulagi near Guadalcanal in the Solomons and the Lae-Salamaua area on Northeast New Guinea would be occupied by the IJN. This move had been urged by the 4th Fleet responsible for the defense of the Mandate, but had not been included in the initial operations.

After the crippling defeats of the Allies and the virtually unopposed occupation of the Bismarcks, the Combined Fleet advocated not only the establishment of bases in the Solomons and on New Guinea, but also the seizure of Port Moresby on the south coast of Papua with the following goals:

- the acquisition of airbases to strengthen the southern defenses and allow expanded aerial reconnaissance to detect enemy naval forces approaching from the southeast;
- depriving the enemy of base areas, preventing their use in any counteroffensive;
- using control of these areas to press against northeast Australia, and hamper its use as a base in any counteroffensive.

An agreement between the IJA and IJN was effected on January 29, and IGHQ issued the following operational orders:

1. Operational objectives: to secure strategic points in the Solomons and Northeast New Guinea in order to cut communications between them and Australia, and to neutralize the waters north of Australia.
2. Operational plan: the IJA and IJN would jointly secure the Lae-Salamaua area and then seize Port Moresby, while the IJN would unilaterally secure key points in the Solomons.
3. Employed strength: the 4th Fleet would provide SNLF and guard forces, and the IJA would commit the South Seas Detachment.
4. Operational outline: to be jointly developed by the IJN and IJA. An operational agreement was concluded between 4th Fleet and the South Seas Detachment on February 16.
5. Land defense: the IJN would be responsible for Tulagi and Lae-Salamaua, and the IJA responsible for Port Moresby.

More ambitious plans

The IJN in particular urged that offensive operations be continued, rather than shifting to the defensive and waiting for the enemy to build his strength—what the Combined Fleet referred to as "negative policies." Such inaction, it was argued, would negate the initial victories and prolong the war. It was essential for Japan to end the war as soon as possible because of its limited resources and forces, and because of the threat posed by the Soviet Union. The IJA wished to conclude the war in China and avoid committing additional forces to the Pacific. The IJA felt no need to advance further, preferring to secure what had been gained. They felt that securing more advanced positions served only to protect over-extended naval bases. The IJN maintained such movements were essential for cutting the Southern Lifeline through the South Pacific, through

An Isuzu 1-ton cargo truck abandoned by IJN construction troops on Guadalcanal. A great deal of construction equipment, supplies, and rations were abandoned by the Japanese. The US Marines made good use of them; when the invasion fleet departed, they were left short of these items.

Japanese supplies and munitions were often too poorly packaged to protect them from the harsh tropical climate. Munitions packaging was improved somewhat from 1943. (Manjiro Terauchi)

which aircraft, men, fuel, and *matériel* flowed from the United States to Australia. The IJN also advocated invading northern Australia, an idea adamantly opposed by the IJA as far too ambitious and beyond the scope of available resources, especially with regard to supplying the invasion force. Further discussions on Australia were withheld. The IJN even suggested plans to seize Hawaii and to land on the western coast of America.

On April 28 a compromise plan was agreed. The invasions of New Caledonia, Fiji, and the Samoas were approved in order to cut the Southern Lifeline. Shortly after, the IJN proposed that Midway be included. The Midway operation, which also included seizing the western Aleutian islands off Alaska, would be conducted in June just prior to the other invasions in the hope of drawing the revitalized Pacific Fleet into a decisive engagement and eliminating it as a threat. The IJN also ordered the seizure of Nauru and the Ocean Islands by 4th Fleet in May, but these operations were not conducted until August. New Caledonia, Fiji, and the Samoas would be seized in July and August by the newly established 17th Army supported by Combined Fleet elements, 2d Fleet, and 11th Air Fleet. The New Caledonia force would assemble at Rabaul in late June and the Fiji and Samoa forces at Truk in early July.

The launch of these operations with the attempt on Midway would prove to be the turning point of the war against Japan, and lead to vicious battles fought in the Solomons, the Bismarcks, and on New Guinea's north coast.

2d Division	Raised in 1870, it fought in the Sino–Japanese and Russo–Japanese wars. It deployed to Manchuria in the 1930s, was soon fighting in North China, and then fought the Soviets in Manchuria in 1939. It returned to Japan in 1940 and departed again in January 1942, arriving on Java in March where it helped complete the operation. Aoba Detachment (4th Infantry) was assigned to the 17th Army at Davao, Mindanao in May. The division assembled on Java and moved to Rabaul in September. It landed on Guadalcanal in October and had largely been destroyed by February 1943. Remnants were sent to Rabaul and then to the Philippines, where it was rebuilt; from November 1943, it spent the rest of the war in Southeast Asia. Commander: LtGen Maruyama Masao.
38th Division	Raised at Nagoya, Japan in February 1939, it deployed to China in December of that year. It seized Hong Kong and then sent regiments to Java, Sumatra, Timor, and other NEI islands. It assembled on Java in late 1942 and moved to Rabaul in October. Small elements were sent to Buna in November, where they were destroyed. In October part of the division was deployed to Guadalcanal, with some elements lost at sea or forced to return to Rabaul. Elements on Guadalcanal had mostly been destroyed by February 1943. It was rebuilt at Rabaul, from which point it remained understrength. The 229th Infantry was destroyed on New Georgia in July and August. Commander: LtGen Sano Tadayoshi.

 (continued on page 11)

35th Infantry Brigade	The brigade (aka Kawaguchi Detachment, or "Force," as it was known in Allied documents) was detached from the 18th Division. The division was activated in 1905 and deactivated in 1925. It was reactivated in 1937 in Kurume, Japan as a square division with the 23d and 35th Infantry brigades, the latter with the 114th and 124th Infantry. The division conducted extensive operations in China from 1937–41. It landed in Malaya in December 1941 and fought there and in Burma, where it remained for the rest of the war. The 35th Infantry Brigade with the 124th Infantry was detached in December 1941 in Canton and fought on Borneo. It went to Cebu, Philippines in March 1942, then Davao, Mindanao in April, then Palau in June. It was on standby for New Guinea, but instead deployed to Guadalcanal in August and by February 1943 had been destroyed. The remnants of the 124th Infantry were rebuilt on Truk and the brigade disbanded. The regiment was sent to Burma and assigned to the new 31st Division. Commander: MajGen Kawaguchi Kiyotake.
5th Division	Organized in 1873, it remained a square division at the beginning of the war and was partly motorized, as well as amphibious trained. It fought in the Sino–Japanese and Russo–Japanese wars. It deployed to China in 1937, fighting there until September 1940, when it moved to Indochina. It conducted brief operations in China and then moved to Hainan Island off South China before landing in Thailand. From late 1942 it occupied and garrisoned various small islands in the NEI. The 41st Infantry was detached and fought on Panay and Mindanao in the Philippines, and then on New Guinea, where it was partly destroyed. It was reassigned to the 30th Division. Commander: LtGen Matsui Takuro.
6th Division	The division was raised in 1870 and fought in the Sino–Japanese and Russo–Japanese wars. It served in China, seeing extensive action from 1937 until it was deployed to Truk in December 1942. Its 13th Infantry fought on New Georgia from July to September 1943, before being evacuated to neighboring Kolombangara and then to Truk. The division was sent to Bougainville in December where it saw heavy action and remained there through the war. Commander: LtGen Kanda Masatane.
17th Division	The division was organized in 1905, and deactivated in 1925. It was reactivated in 1938 at Himeji, Japan and sent to China; it saw extensive action there until August 1943, when it deployed to Truk, and then to Rabaul between October and November. It saw heavy action on western New Britain and elements deployed to Bougainville. From early 1944 it was located at Rabaul and remained there for the rest of the war. Commander: LtGen Sakai Yashushi.
65th Brigade	This brigade was raised at Hiroshima, Japan in early 1941 from the 65th Independent Infantry Group. It was sent to Formosa and landed on Luzon in December 1941. It fought there and remained on the island until December 1942 when one regiment and the HQ were sent to Rabaul and the other regiments elsewhere. The brigade was dissolved in late 1943 after its units were absorbed into others. Commander: MajGen Naka Akira.
21st Independent Mixed Brigade	The 21st IMB was organized in January 1941 around the 170th Infantry, 104th Division at Osaka, Japan. It served as an occupation force in Indochina in early 1942 and was then sent to Malaya, and then Rabaul in November. Part of the brigade was destroyed on New Guinea after landing in December. II/170 was stationed on Wake and absorbed into 13th Independent Infantry Regiment. The brigade was deactivated in July 1943. Commander: MajGen Yamagata Yikao (aka Tsuyuo).
20th Division	Activated in 1919 in Korea, it remained there until sent to China in 1937. It returned to Korea in 1939 and then deployed to Madang, Northeast New Guinea in February 1943. This was the one division deployed to the Southeast Area without recent prior combat experience. It fought there, dwindling away until the war's end. Commander: LtGen Katagiri Shigeru.
41st Division	The division was raised in 1939 in Utsunomiya, Japan. It was soon sent to China, but in February 1943 it deployed to Palau, then Wewak in Northeast New Guinea. It was virtually destroyed, but remained active to the war's end. Commander: LtGen Mano Goro.
51st Division	The 51st was organized in 1940 in Kanazawa, Japan. It was deployed to Manchuria in 1941 and then to China. In November 1942 it deployed to Palau, then Rabaul in December. Part of the division was lost en route to New Guinea in March 1943 during the Battle of the Bismarck Sea. Elements of the division were sent to New Georgia and then the division reassembled in the Lae-Salamaua area between March and May 1943. It was virtually destroyed in New Guinea and surrendered at war's end. Commander: MajGen Nakano Hidemitau.

Unit organization

A brief "refresher" is provided here on IJA unit structure. The ascending hierarchy of IJA units was as follows: section (squad), platoon, company, battalion, regiment, brigade, division, army (a corps-equivalent formation), and area army. A "group" was usually a brigade-equivalent unit. Artillery used the term "company" rather than "battery." Infantry and artillery regiments consisted of three organic battalions designated by Roman numbers (I–III), but tank, reconnaissance, cavalry, engineer, shipping engineer, signal, and many transport regiments were actually of battalion size and were composed of only three to five companies. In this volume, "regiment" is usually deleted from a regiment's designation; for example, the term "78th Infantry" is used, as opposed to "78th Infantry Regiment." A "unit" (*Tai* or *Butai*) could range in size from a platoon to a battalion or larger support unit. Most units ranging from Section to Area Army were designated by Latin numbers; in Japanese, the 21st Independent Mixed Brigade, for example, would be entitled *Dai 21 Dokuritsu Konset Ryodan*, with "Dai" being the prefix identifying ordinal numbers. A few newly numbered armies (*Gun*) were organized[1]. Numbered area armies (*Homengun*) were raised in the summer of 1942 to control one to four armies, a newly formed air army, and service units and depots in operational areas.

The IJA widely employed "detachments" (*Shitai*) built around an infantry group (most divisions possessed an infantry group to control their three infantry regiments); alternatively, one of a square division's two brigade headquarters would be detached in the same role. To this were added an infantry regiment, artillery battalion, engineer company, medical unit, and other support units. However, such detachments could be organized in a very different manner, being tailored to a specific mission. Special detachments (*Shitai*) were usually named after the commander and were referred to as "detachments" or "forces" by the Allies. They could also be assigned a name describing their position in the line (Right or Left Flank Unit) or mission (Raiding or Occupation Force).

Several unit terms require additional explanation. Units designated "line-of-communications" (*Heitan*, hereafter LoC) were rear service and administrative units, usually assigned to LoC sector units (*Heitan Chikutai*). These were administrative headquarters responsible for rear area service in specific sectors. Assigned units included LoC motor transport units, LoC hospitals, duty companies, and various depots as well as LoC garrison units. "Duty" (*Kimmu*) companies, which could be designated land, sea, construction, or LoC duty, were stevedore or general labor units. There were also LoC garrison units used for security; these were essentially small infantry battalions.

Japanese tables of organization were provided in several forms, with differing manpower and equipment levels, and were also structured for specific areas. The Japanese, for example, provided for three variants of triangular infantry divisions, but captured documents of deployed units showed that none were organized exactly as per the official variants. Many types of units were provided with man-packed, packhorse, horse-drawn, or, in rare instances, partly motorized tables of organization. This, coupled with shortages and local modifications, mean that deployed units demonstrated a very broad variety of internal structures and strengths. The production of crew-served weapons

---

1 Armies were designated with Latin numbers, but Australian sources often designated them using Roman numbers, equating them to Western corps equivalents.

could not keep pace with the need to equip new units and replace combat losses, and this resulted in the use of substitute weapons. In contrast, some units deployed with additional weapons. Divisions and independent brigades were as much as 20 percent below authorized strength due to rear-area detachments, hospitalization, attending schools and courses, secondment to higher commands, criminal charges, and so on. The battalions that were detached from certain divisions in order to man South Seas, garrison, and replacement units were usually at or near full strength. These battalions were detached from divisions in China, Manchuria, Korea, and Japan and were made up to strength prior to deployment by drawing personnel and equipment from other divisional units. The lost battalions were later reorganized with replacement recruits and cadres drawn from other divisional units.

Unit designation practices have already been discussed in the first volume (Battle Orders 9), but besides traditional military designations the IJA also made extensive use of code names and numbers. These were usually used together, served as postal codes, and identified units in communications traffic and shipping orders. Determining which codes were assigned to which units was critical for Allied intelligence when deciphering signal intercepts. For the most part, units never changed code names and numbers. Code names were assigned to armies, divisions, independent brigades, and shipping engineer units, and used single or compound characters. Some of these characters had two meanings and were identified by Allied intelligence with both; for example, Southern Army was identified as "I/Odosu 1160". Code numbers were assigned to all units with separate identities including higher headquarters, divisions, brigades and non-division brigades, independent regiments, battalions, companies, units, and the like. Most units were assigned four- or five-digit codes, although some in Manchuria (the first to be assigned code numbers) had two- and three-digit codes. When a unit was relocated to another theater, it would more often than not retain its number, but the preceding code name would change to that of the new command. Units in Manchuria (code named Manshu) with two- or three-digit numbers received a new four-digit number if deployed elsewhere, while those with four-digit numbers retained them. The 2d Division fighting on Guadalcanal was coded Isamu 1339 with its assigned units numbered between 1301 and 1310 (infantry regiments: 4th—1301; 16th—1302; 29th—1303). Other divisions sometimes had mixed code numbers if the regiments were from other divisions. The 2d Division was also commonly known as the "Sendai Division," being nicknamed after its home prefecture, a common practice among permanent divisions.

Table 1: Army code names and numbers		
Southern Area, 1942–44		
Army	**Code name**	**Number**
Southern Army	I/Odosu	1160
2d Area Army	Kagayku/Teru	16300
8th Area Army	Go	7960
2d Army	Sei/Ikioi	16400
16th Army	Osamu/Chi/Haru	1602
17th Army	Oki	9811
18th Army	Mo	7910
19th Army	Ken/Katashi	9450
25th Army	Tomi	9990
37th Army	Neda	9801

On Guadalcanal and New Guinea, where Japanese units rapidly dwindled in strength, they retained their designations regardless of their true size. Companies would be consolidated and then disappear as battalions fell below 100 men. They too would evaporate as battalions fell to only dozens of men and regiments to between 100 and 200 effective soldiers. In some cases, divisions retained their identity despite having less than 2,000 men.

Infantry divisions

After the initial conquests the few remaining square infantry divisions (5th, 13th, 18th, 19th, 20th, and 116th) were triangularized, losing a regiment and their two brigade headquarters. The latter often became an independent brigade headquarters and the lost regiments were reassigned to the new 30th and 31st divisions in 1943.

The more common standard B, or *Otsu*, triangular infantry division of 20,000 troops has already been discussed in the previous volume (Battle Orders 9). The standard B divisions committed to the Southern Operation in 1941–42 included the 4th, 16th, 21st, 33d, 38th, 55th, and 56th. The 5th and 18th were square divisions, which were converted to standard B divisions in early 1942 and early 1943 respectively. The 2d and Guards divisions were strengthened standard A divisions. Additional divisions were committed to the Southern Area in 1942–43 with the 20th and 51st being standard A and the 6th, 17th, and 41st being standard B.

Although similar to the standard B division, the standard A, or *Ko*, division retained an infantry group headquarters, and possessed an artillery group headquarters. The inclusion of the artillery group, to supplement the planning and fire-control capabilities of the organic artillery regiment, was a result of the lessons learned fighting the Soviets in Manchuria in 1939. In fact, most standard A divisions were assigned to the Kwantung Army in Manchuria, although a few served with the China Expeditionary Army. While there were variations in the assigned units of standard A divisions, as there were in most divisions, they were generally organized as per the other divisions, but with a strength of up to 24,600 troops. The standard A infantry regiment was similar to the standard B, but with minor differences and an increased total strength of 4,831 troops and over 700 horses.

Table 2: Standard A infantry regiment

	Strength	Main weapons
Regimental HQ with train	198	4 x LMGs
Regimental infantry gun company	170	4 x 7.5cm infantry guns
Regimental antitank company	130	6 x 3.7cm AT guns
Regimental signal company	130	
Infantry battalion (x 3):	1,401	
Battalion HQ with train	177	I x LMG
Rifle company (x 4)	205	9 x LMGs, 9 x grenade dischargers
Battalion machine gun company	174	12 x HMGs
Battalion gun company	230	4 x 7cm infantry guns, 8 x 2cm AT rifles

Attachments:

Artillery battalion (occasionally)

Engineer company from divisional engineer regiment

Regimental medical unit from divisional medical service

Signal sections from divisional signal unit

Labor unit (common, often formed from regimental assets)

Table 3: Southeast area divisions

Division	Infantry regts	Artillery regt	Recon/Cavalry regt	Engineer regt	Transport regt
2d	4, 16, 29	2 FA	2 Recon	2	2
5th	11, 21, 42	5 FA	5 Recon	5	5
6th	13, 23, 45	6 FA	6 Cavalry	6	6
17th	53, 54, 81	23 FA	Tankette Co[1]	17	17
20th	78, 79, 80	26 FA[2]	20 Recon	20	20
38th	228, 229, 230	38 Mountain	Tankette Co[1]	38	38
41st	237, 238, 239	41 Mountain	—	41	41
51st	66, 102, 115	14 FA[2]	51 Recon	51	51

Notes: All divisions possessed an Infantry Group HQ.
[1] Designated, for example, Tankette Company, 17th Infantry Group.
[2] Possessed an Artillery Group HQ.

Besides the triangular or "three units" division (*San-tan-i Shidan* or *3 Tani Shidan*) and square or "four units" division (*Yon-tan-i Shidan* or *4 Tani Shidan*), the IJA also fielded what the Allies called the "brigaded" or "special" division for occupation and anti-bandit duty in China, though some were later raised elsewhere. The IJA referred to these as security divisions (*chian shidan*), though "security" was not included in their designations. Even following the outbreak of the Pacific War, Japan raised only seven additional infantry divisions in early 1942; six were security divisions created by expanding existing IMBs. While these divisions consisted of two infantry brigades, they were not square divisions in that they did not possess two battalions with two infantry regiments each. Instead, the brigades each comprised four large independent infantry brigades (IIBs, *Dokuritsu Hohei Daitai*), each with five rifle companies. Their strength was some 12,000 troops though some battalions had fewer companies, four or even three. Rifle strength was high, but they lacked artillery and reconnaissance units and engineer, transport, signal, and medical support was much reduced. A standard division might be authorized up to 7,500 horses, but a more or less static brigaded division had only 2,000 or less.

Table 4: example standard C security ("brigaded") division, 1942

Division HQ	250
Infantry brigade (x 2)	
Brigade HQ	
Independent infantry battalion (x 4)	1,220
Battalion HQ	
Rifle company (x 5)	
Machine gun company	
Infantry gun company	
Engineer unit	250
Transport unit	800
Signal unit	140
Medical unit	500

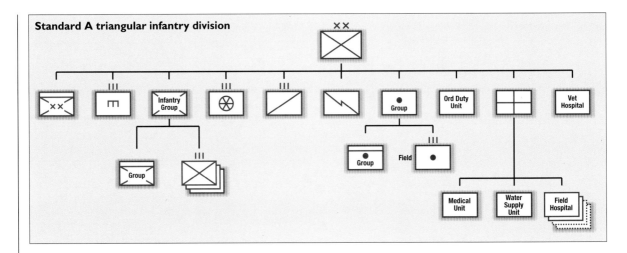

Standard A triangular infantry division

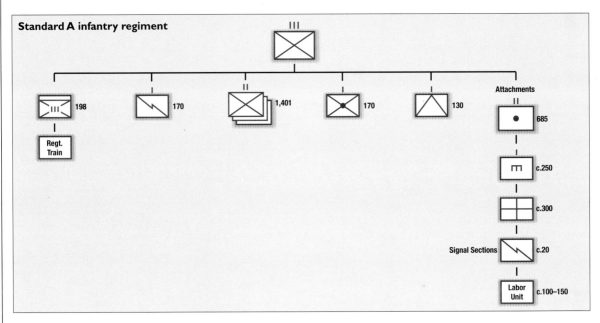

Standard A infantry regiment

In addition to the six security divisions, the 1st–3d tank divisions (*Sensha Shidan*) were raised. Tank divisions were designated, for example, *Sensha dai 1 Shidan*, or "Tank 1st Division." All were activated in Manchuria in late 1942 using existing battalion-size tank regiments and two tank group headquarters. The two-regiment tank group proved unsuited to command, control, and combat and service support. Assigned to the Kwantung Army, they were subordinate to the Tank Army formed at the same time, which was subsequently inactivated. The divisions originally had two brigades, but were triangularized in 1944. The Japanese were provided with the organization and doctrine employed by the German Panzer force and their tank division structure was loosely based on that of the Panzer divisions. These divisions will be discussed in a forthcoming Battle Orders title.

Brigade equivalents
The IJA fielded a number of brigade-equivalent units, including independent mixed brigades, independent infantry brigades, independent infantry groups, independent mixed regiments, and independent infantry regiments. The differences between these units were often minor, although their strength could

Heavy machine gun platoon, battalion machine gun company

Platoon headquarters

a   b

Legend

a	Platoon commander, lieutenant (pistol)
b	Liaison sergeant (rifle)
c	Section leader, sergeant (pistol)
1	Assistant section leader/runner, corporal (pistol)
2	Loader, lance corporal (pistol)

3	Assistant loader, superior private (pistol)
4	Gunner, private first class (pistol)
5–7	Ammunition bearer (unarmed)
8	Ammunition bearer (rifle)
9–10	Horse handler/ammunition bearer (unarmed)

1st heavy machine gun section

c   1   2   3   4   5   6   7   8   9   10

2d heavy machine gun section

c   1   2   3   4   5   6   7   8   9   10

3d heavy machine gun section

c   1   2   3   4   5   6   7   8   9   10

4th heavy machine gun section

c   1   2   3   4   5   6   7   8   9   10

Notes: In the Pacific the two pack horses and handlers were removed, and most "unarmed" men were provided with rifles.

Standard C Security ("Brigaded") Division, 1942

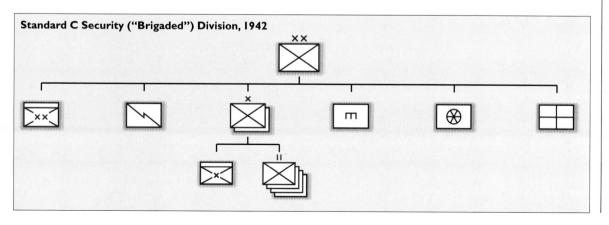

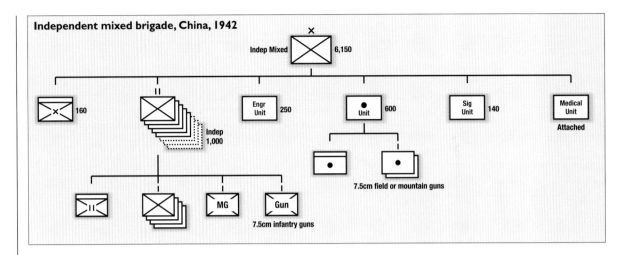

Independent mixed brigade, China, 1942

Indep Mixed 6,150 · 160 · Indep 1,000 · Engr Unit 250 · Unit 600 · Sig Unit 140 · Medical Unit Attached · MG · Gun · 7.5cm infantry guns · 7.5cm field or mountain guns

vary considerably due to their status and assigned missions. The major differences in the organization of brigade-equivalent units lay in the numbers and types of assigned support units. These were important units and the Japanese fielded as many or even more brigade-equivalent units than they did divisions through 1944. Most armies employing brigades opted for more divisions.

Independent mixed brigades (*Dokuritsu Konset Ryodan*) were mainly intended for occupation duty and LoC security, and were extensively employed in China. Many armies had one IMB or more to secure their rear area. They were soon employed elsewhere in conquered territories in similar roles, but as operational circumstances changed many found themselves committed to frontline combat. Others were strengthened with replacements and expanded to divisions.

IMBs consisted of three to six IIBs, each with three or four rifle companies. Those in China usually had four to six four-company, 1,000-man IIBs. An alternative type had three to six 930-man, four-company battalions; while the type with three-rifle company IIBs had only 580-man battalions, but could consist of up to eight IIBs. Brigade strength varied from 9,000–11,000 troops. Supporting units varied between the different main types of IMBs. They usually had a battalion-size artillery unit of twelve 7.5cm howitzers, a large company-size engineer unit, and a company-size signal unit. Many IMBs were distinctly organized, though, with additional attachments. The 21st IMB and 65th Brigade were both unique, the 21st having a three-battalion infantry regiment and the 65th having three, two-battalion regiments. The modern IMBs originated in about 1933, when divisions based in Japan dispatched brigades of mixed infantry and artillery to China for temporary duty.

Independent infantry brigades (*Dokuritsu Hohei Ryodan*) had four independent infantry battalions and no artillery or other supporting units other than a small signal unit. Few were deployed. Independent infantry groups (*Dokuritsu Hoheidan*) were fielded with three divisional-type infantry regiments and no support units. They later provided the cadre for new divisions, as did independent infantry brigades. A small number of independent mixed regiments (*Dokuritsu Konset Rentai*), with an attached artillery unit, and independent infantry regiments (*Dokuritsu Hohei Rentai*), without artillery or other support, were also organized. Some of these were used as island garrison forces, but most were reassigned to new divisions.

The Guards divisions

The three Guards divisions (*Konoe Shidan*) were manned by specially selected, Class A personnel, for whom the minimum height was 1.52m (5ft). Troops selected for the Guards infantry and cavalry regiments were taller. The original Guards Division was activated in 1867 in Tokyo, and grew in size over the years. As a square division its 2d Guards Brigade (*Dai 2 Konoe Ryodan*) containing the 3d and 4th Guards Infantry regiments was sent to Shanghai and then Southern China in 1940 to gain combat experience. In June 1941 the 1st Guards Brigade and its 1st and 2d Guards Infantry were detached from the division and reorganized as the Guards Mixed Brigade (*Konoe Konset Ryodan*), which was to remain in Tokyo. The 2d Brigade, now on Hainan Island off China's south coast, became the new Guards Division, a standard A triangular division, augmented by the new 5th Guards Infantry. The remainder of the division assembled on Hainan while the Guards Mixed Brigade continued to protect the Imperial family. In July 1941 the Guards Division went to Indochina, then Thailand and Malaya, where it suffered heavy casualties. In March 1942 it was deployed to Medam, northern Sumatra for garrison duty where it remained for the rest of the war. Detachments were dispatched to garrison the Andaman and Nicobar islands northwest of Sumatra in the Indian Ocean. The Guards Division was redesignated the 2d Guards Division in June 1943 when the Guards Mixed Brigade in Tokyo became the 1st Guards Division consisting of the original 1st and 2d and the new 6th Guards Infantry; it also received other units, making it a standard B division. The 3d Guards Division, also standard B, was activated in Tokyo in April 1944 with the 8th–10th Guards Infantry (although no 7th Guards was ever activated).

Mortar and antitank units

The Japanese assigned few mortars to infantry units, relying instead on 7cm battalion and 7.5cm regimental (infantry) guns. Due to the wartime expansion of units and the scarcity of infantry guns, some infantry units, especially IMBs, received mortars. Mortars were mainly assigned to non-divisional units and detached down to infantry battalion level. The 8cm trench mortar units were assigned to the infantry, while heavier mortars (9cm and up) came under the aegis of the artillery. The mortar battalion (*Hakugeki Daitai*) consisted of a headquarters with observation and signal sections. The three mortar companies had a similarly organized headquarters and four platoons, each with a small headquarters and four five-man sections manning a single 9cm mortar. The battalion and each company also had an ammunition train. Some 900 troops manned the 36-mortar unit. The 3d Trench Mortar Battalion assigned to 17th Army was unusual in that its three component 8cm mortar companies were detached from the 1st Independent Mortar Regiment in Manchuria.

Independent antitank battalions (*Dokuritsu Sokushaho Daitai*) and companies (*Dokuritsu Sokushaho Chutai*) could be attached to divisions. A 490-man

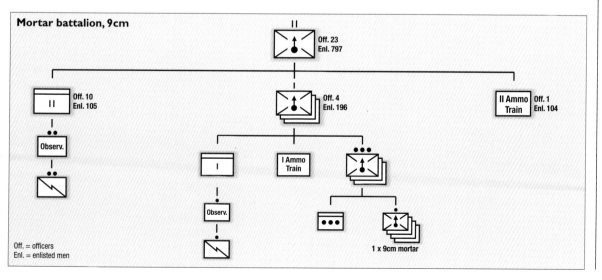

Mortar battalion, 9cm

Off. 23 / Enl. 797

Off. 10 / Enl. 105 — Observ.

Off. 4 / Enl. 196 — I Ammo Train — Observ. — 1 x 9cm mortar

II Ammo Train — Off. 1 / Enl. 104

Off. = officers
Enl. = enlisted men

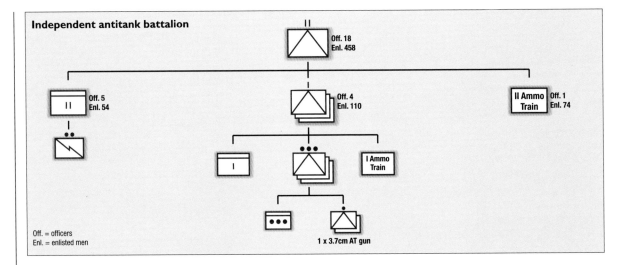

Independent antitank battalion

Off. 18
Enl. 458

Off. 5
Enl. 54

Off. 4
Enl. 110

II Ammo Train
Off. 1
Enl. 74

I Ammo Train

1 x 3.7cm AT gun

Off. = officers
Enl. = enlisted men

battalion had a headquarters plus an ammunition train and three companies. The companies had a headquarters, ammunition platoon, and three two-gun platoons. A gun section operated a 3.7cm gun with an 11-man crew. The 180 or 250-man independent antitank company could be armed with six or eight guns across three or four platoons. Both battalions and companies could be packhorse or motorized with light trucks or tractors. Often, those deployed to the South Seas relied on man-packing.

Artillery units

Non-divisional artillery units included field, mountain, mortar, medium, and heavy artillery types. Only small numbers of independent artillery regiments existed, but there were significant numbers of independent artillery battalions. Most independent regiments had a headquarters, regimental ammunition train, and two battalions rather than the three found in divisional regiments. Independent artillery battalions had a headquarters, ammunition train, and two or three companies depending on type. Most companies possessed four guns, but many heavy companies had only two. Most artillery heavy mortar companies had 12. Heavy artillery regiments, though, possessed only two four-gun companies—in effect making them small battalions.

Independent artillery units were usually assigned to army troops and could be attached to divisions. These units could be horse, truck, or tractor drawn, or pack-horsed. Few independent artillery regiments were deployed to the South Pacific though. The guns, ammunition, and equipment were far too difficult to

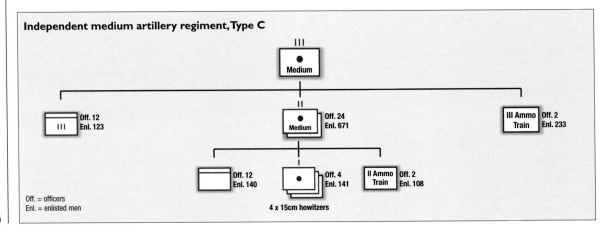

Independent medium artillery regiment, Type C

Medium

Off. 12
Enl. 123

Medium
Off. 24
Enl. 671

III Ammo Train
Off. 2
Enl. 233

Off. 12
Enl. 140

Off. 4
Enl. 141

II Ammo Train
Off. 2
Enl. 108

Off. = officers
Enl. = enlisted men

4 x 15cm howitzers

move on the trackless islands without trucks or horses. They simply could not be manhandled through the jungle. Shipping space and the difficulties of unloading and landing heavy guns under the prevalent threat of air attack were other considerations. Divisional artillery units more often than not remained in the rear, as happened at Buin on Bougainville, Rabaul on New Britain, Truk, and the Palaus. In most cases the Japanese relied on a few small artillery units detached from the divisional regiment and their more portable regimental and battalion guns.

Mountain artillery units were useful in the Pacific because of the lightness of their weapons, and the ability to break them down for man-packing; the 7.5cm Type 94 mountain gun could be disassembled into 11 components.

Guadalcanal saw the heaviest use of artillery by the Japanese in the Southeast Area. It was realized there how difficult it was to move the guns and ammunition and keep them supplied, and how easily they were lost to American counterbattery fire and air attack. The ferocity of Allied counterfire made artillerymen hesitant to fire. It was common for American troops to find abandoned guns and deteriorating ammunition stocks hidden in the jungle near to where they had been landed, and never moved forward. The effectiveness of artillery was limited by low ammunition stocks.

Field artillery, both divisional and non-divisional, was largely horsedrawn. This pre-war photo shows a 7.5cm field gun caisson.

Table 5: artillery ammunition available on Guadalcanal

Weapon	Guns available	Total rounds
7.5cm Type 38 field gun	7	1,370
7.5cm mountain gun[1]	22	150
10cm Type 91 howitzer	4	(unknown)
10cm Type 92 gun	4	742
15cm Type 4 howitzer	4	420
15cm Type 96 howitzer	12	709

Notes
[1] Included Type 41, Type 95, and Bofors m/28 mountain guns. Each gun used a different type of ammunition and none were interchangeable with 7.5cm field guns. It is believed that the 150 rounds were for one type of gun and additional rounds were available for others.

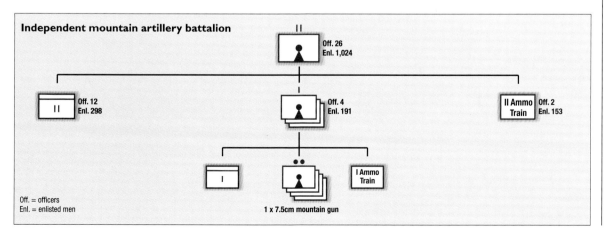

Independent mountain artillery battalion

II — Off. 26 / Enl. 1,024

II — Off. 12 / Enl. 298

Off. 4 / Enl. 191

II Ammo Train — Off. 2 / Enl. 153

I

I Ammo Train

Off. = officers
Enl. = enlisted men

1 x 7.5cm mountain gun

Some independent, non-divisional field artillery units were provided with full-tracked tractor prime-movers, such as this 8-ton Ikegai Type 92 (1932) example. Few of these were deployed to the Pacific though. An artillery unit might have taken with them only part of their authorized tractor complement.

The Type C independent medium artillery regiments (*Dokuritsu Yasen Rentai*) under the 17th Army on Rabaul, which had elements deployed to Guadalcanal, were organized into a headquarters, ammunition train, and two battalions of three companies each, each with four 15cm Type 4 (1915) howitzers. There were supposed to be three 6-ton tractors for each howitzer as a prime mover and to haul ammunition, but nothing near this many were deployed, and none were sent to Guadalcanal. The 21st Medium Artillery Regiment was a Type D unit organized with a headquarters, ammunition train and two battalions with only two four-gun companies each armed with a total of sixteen 10cm Type 82 (1932) guns. These had almost twice the range of the 15cm howitzer—20,000 yards as opposed to 10,800 yards. The 21st was supposed to have 42 five-ton tractors, but once again few were deployed. It is common for medium regiments to be identified as "heavy" in certain references.

The 10th Independent Mountain Artillery Regiment (*Dai 10 Dokuritsu Yasen Juhohei Rentai*) had a headquarters, ammunition train, and two battalions with three four-gun companies armed with a total of twenty-four 7.5cm Type 94 (1934) mountain guns. The 20th Independent Mountain Artillery Battalion (*Dai 20 Dokuritsu Yasen Juhohei Daitai*) equated to one of the regiment's battalions. These units deployed without horses and relied solely on manpower.

The 17th Army controlled its artillery units through the 9th Artillery Command (*Dai 9 Hohei Shireibu*) at Rabaul. The 18th Army on Eastern New Guinea had no artillery units other than those assigned to its three divisions. In January 1944 IGHQ decided to allot the 2d Area Army three additional medium or heavy artillery regiments, but these were never sent.

Antiaircraft units

While units in the Solomons and New Guinea lacked artillery, the same cannot be said of the antiaircraft units. The 18th Army, which had no army-level artillery and little in its divisions, was assigned six antiaircraft battalions, four antiaircraft companies, and two machine cannon companies. Antiaircraft units were easier to deploy and supply with ammunition. They were usually delivered near to where they were supposed to defend airfields and supply bases, and remained there. Such areas were usually adjacent to the coast, which meant the guns only had to be moved a short distance prior to being dug in, and ammunition could be stockpiled near to where it was delivered by ship or barge.

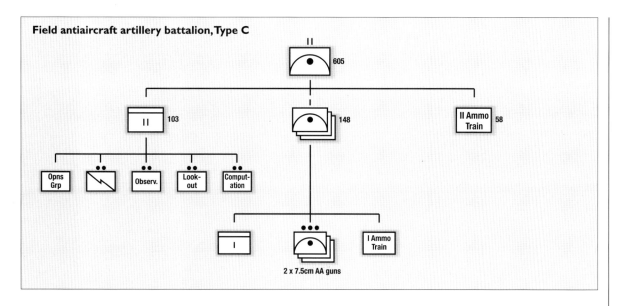

Field antiaircraft artillery battalion, Type C

The IJA fielded a bewildering array of antiaircraft units, with little to distinguish them apart either organizationally or in terms of armament. The most common type found in operational areas was the field antiaircraft artillery battalion (*Yasen Koshabo Daitai*). This unit type was intended for deployment overseas, and possessed more tactical mobility than independent antiaircraft defense and antiaircraft artillery battalions, which mostly remained in Japan. It had a headquarters, ammunition train, and three companies. The field antiaircraft artillery battalion was divided into Type A battalions, with sufficient mobility to move all its weapons and equipment simultaneously, and Type B and C semi-mobile battalions with half the number of vehicles. Type A and C battalions had eighteen 7.5cm AA guns (six per company), while the Type B had only four per company. Their strength was 450, 515, and 695 men respectively. The Type C was the most common in the Pacific.

Independent field antiaircraft artillery companies (*Dokuritsu Yasen Koshabo Chutai*) were also widely deployed and had four 7.5cm guns. The battalion and company headquarters were divided into signal, observation, lookout, and

A 2.5-ton Nissan 80 truck mounting a 7.7mm Nambu Type 92 (1932) HMG on an antiaircraft adapter mount. The Nissan 80 was the first mass-produced truck in Japan. Although it was civilian-designed and had only two-wheel drive, it was used extensively by the IJA.

computation sections, and there was a machine gun section in each company. Several independent field searchlight companies (*Dokuritsu Yasen Shoku Chutai*) were deployed in New Guinea and the NEI; each had six searchlights.

Field machine cannon companies (*Yasen Kikanho Chutai*) were of two types. The Type A had six each of the 2cm Type 98 (1938) machine cannon and the 13.2mm Type 93 (1933) machine gun, and consisted of 155 men organized into three platoons with two guns of each of these calibers. The Type B company had only six 2cm cannons in two three-gun platoons.

The Air Services

Both the IJA and IJN possessed their own air services, respectively called the *Teikoku Rikugun Kokutai* and the *Teikoku Kaigun Kokutai*. These air arms developed independently, and had different missions, aircraft models, and tactics. The IJA Air Service was solely intended to support the ground forces, and possessed little in the way of strategic capability. Bombers were comparatively short ranged, and most troop transport was provided by contracted commercial airlines. Transport units were increased during the war along with other types of flying units, but remained insufficient for the tasks, as did the long-range bomber units. Aerial resupply by parachute was usually conducted by bombers, which distracted them from their primary role.

The IJN Air Service had a broader outlook and mission. It formed the fleet air arm, and provided coastal defense, antisubmarine warfare capabilities, convoy escort and long-range maritime reconnaissance duties, as well as supporting expeditionary operations. Besides the highly trained carrier flying units (1st Air Fleet), the IJN possessed an even larger land-based air force (11th Air Fleet) with fighters, dive-bombers, torpedo-bombers, attack, reconnaissance, and heavy bombers. This included mobile units with reconnaissance-bomber seaplanes and floatplane fighters capable of operating from advanced bases without the need for airstrips. Most Japanese air activity over the Solomons and New Guinea was conducted by the IJN Air Service. There was little coordination between the IJA and IJN air services.

Foreign observations during the 1939 border war with the USSR concluded that the IJA Air Service was not as well trained as the IJN's. IJA training focused on the pilots, and aircrew training was accomplished largely within units. The IJN provided detailed training to aircrews, bombardiers, navigators, signalmen, gunners, and flight engineers. The IJN produced almost three times the number of pilots per year that the IJA did. The IJA conducted little over-water training and most of its aircraft were short ranged; for example, in 1941 its bombers had only a 500-mile range. The reason for this was that it was only tasked with supporting ground forces from behind-the-lines airfields. The IJN, on the other hand, conducted extensive over-water training out to 800 miles; its strategic mission was to control narrow seas and maritime "chokepoints," as well as to defend the Mandate's widespread islands. The IJN also planned to expand the perimeter of the Empire, which would require long-range aircraft that could operate over water. The IJA Air Service had more combat experience though; some 50 percent of the pilots had operated in China or against the USSR. In contrast, only 10 percent of IJN pilots had combat experience in China.

While often discounted by foreign analysts, the Japanese air forces were well-trained, experienced, and possessed adequate aircraft. They were unable to replace airframe and aircrew losses sufficiently, and did not have the resources and time to develop more effective aircraft to counter the growing Allied air capabilities from 1943. The IJA and IJN also competed for construction materials and factory workloads, and failed to share lessons learned and research information. The fatal flaw in Japanese air planning was to ignore American production capabilities and its ability to train more than sufficient numbers of aircrew. For example, in 1941 Japan produced fewer than 5,100 aircraft and 3,000 pilots, while the US, to support the rapid pre-war expansion of its own armed forces and the needs of Great Britain, turned out almost 20,000 aircraft and 11,000 Army pilots. The China Incident in 1937 did lead to an expansion of the Air Service, but it was a slow process. The IJA possessed only 1,500 frontline combat aircraft on December 8, 1941: 550 fighters (*Sentoki*), 660 light (*Keibaku*) and heavy (*Jubku*) bombers (often referred to as "medium bombers"), and 290 reconnaissance (*Teisatsuki*) aircraft. Transport, liaison, trainer, and research aircraft were additional to these figures.

The IJA Air Service did not directly come under the control of any one headquarters. Operational control was the responsibility of the Chief of the General Staff; the War Ministry was responsible for personnel and administration through the Inspector General of Aviation (*Koku Sokambu*); and the Inspector General of Military Training oversaw flying unit training.

The basic operating unit of the IJA Air Service was the flying regiment (*Hiko Sentai*) with two to four flying companies (*Hiko Chutai*) all with a common type of aircraft[2]. Fighter regiments usually had three companies, occasionally four, and bomber and reconnaissance regiments only two. Flying companies were divided into three or four sections (*Shotai*) of three aircraft. There were several aircraft in the flying regiment headquarters (*Hiko Sentai Hombu*) and three or so spare aircraft for each company; bomber units had fewer spares. The flying regiment was commanded by a lieutenant colonel or major, and might have either 27 or 36 aircraft at full strength plus about one-third of this number comprising spare and headquarters aircraft[3].

A flying brigade (*Hikodan*) had two or three flying regiments under a colonel or major general, plus an air sector headquarters. The component regiments might be all of one type, but it was common to mix them—for example, a light bomber and two fighter regiments plus a small reconnaissance unit and a brigade headquarters (*Shireibu Hikodan*). The air sector headquarters (*Koku Chiku Shireibu*) provided all services, fuel, stores, maintenance, and administrative support to the brigade's units. This was provided through an airfield battalion (*Hikojo Daitai*) or company (*Hikojo Chutai*) matched with each regiment. They provided aircraft maintenance, supply services, and airfield security and were organized for the specific type of aircraft used by the regiment they supported.

Specialized independent flying units (*Dokuritsu Hikotai*) and companies (*Dokuritsu Hiko Chutai*) could be assigned directly to flying brigades, flying divisions, or higher commands. These included reconnaissance, meteorological, and other special duty units.

The early-war flying group (*Hiko Shudan*) was redesignated a flying division (*Hiko Shidan*) in mid 1942. A major general or lieutenant general commanded a division, which in theory consisted of two or three flying brigades.

Table 6: IJA Air Service flying units			
English/abbreviation	**Japanese**	**US equivalent**	**Commonwealth equivalent**
Section	*Shotai*	Flight	Flight
Flying company (FC)	*Hiko Chutai*	Squadron	Squadron
Flying unit (FM)	*Hikotai/FM*	Squadron	Squadron
Flying regiment (FR)	*Hiko Sentai*	Group	Wing
Flying brigade (FB)	*Hikodan*	Wing	Group
Flying division (FD)	*Hiko Shidan*	Air division	—
Air army (FA)	*Kokugun*	Numbered air force	Command

---

2 Many english-language sources incorrectly translate *Chutai* as "squadron" and *Hiko* as "air."
3 The term flying battalion (*Hiko Daitai*) is sometimes encountered, but in 1938 this echelon was eliminated and most independent flying battalions were redesignated as regiments.

Composition varied greatly in practice, with two to four brigades as well as some flying regiments and independent flying units and companies directly under divisional control. Flying divisions also had an air intelligence regiment or unit (*Koku Joho Rentai* or *Tai*), an air signal regiment or unit (*Koku Tsushin Rentai* or *Tai*), airfield construction units (*Yasen Hikojo Setteitai*), and miscellaneous service units. The 1st–3d Air Armies (*Kokugun*) were established in June and July 1942, and the 4th in July 1943, in order to control air units assigned to the new area armies. Flying units were supported by a variety of repair depots, and aircraft repair, navigation aid, and supply units.

IJN Air Service units predominated in the South Pacific, and thus a brief discussion needs to be allocated to them here. They were organized into companies (*Chutai*), air groups (*Kokutai*), air flotillas (*Koku Sentai*), and air fleets (*Koku Kantai*), and had an extremely flexible structure. The IJN had 1,670 combat aircraft.

Table 7: IJA Air Service deployment, July 1942

Home Islands and Manchuria	1st Air Army
	17th, 18th, 19th, 20th Flying divisions
Manchukuo	2d Air Army
	2d, 6th, 7th, 8th Flying divisions
	4th Air Army
	4th, 9th, 10th, 13th Flying divisions
China	3d Flying Division
Southern Front	3d Air Army
Burma	4th Flying Brigade
Malaya	7th Flying Brigade
Java	Three flying regiments of 3d Flying Brigade
Sumatra	Two flying regiments of 12th Flying Brigade
Indochina	Two flying regiments
Philippines	Three flying regiments
New Guinea and Rabaul	6th Air Division

Doctrine and tactics

The IJA was entirely oriented to the offensive, and sought a decisive battle to defeat the Allies. Doctrine and tactics have already been discussed in detail in the preceding volume *Conquest of the Pacific 1941–42* (Battle Orders 9), but the key attributes of Japanese tactics are briefly summarized below:

- A strong preference for offensive movement, and an abhorrence of defense.
- A heavy reliance on "strength of will"—*seishin*.
- An emphasis on surprise, rapid movement, commanders operating well forward, and simple plans.
- A preference for envelopment or encirclement of the enemy rather than frontal attacks.
- A desire to advance in two or three columns, to allow envelopment or encirclement.

In spite of their hatred of it, the Japanese soon found themselves on the defensive tactically, operationally, and strategically. However, at upper-echelon levels, commanders were slow to accept this. They initially attempted to conduct the defense aggressively through counterattacks and counter-offensives. Counterlandings—amphibious landings on the enemy's established beachheads—were attempted in some instances.

In order to understand the tactics employed by the Japanese, the tactical environment in the Solomons and on New Guinea must first be examined. The Solomons are a double chain of almost 1,000 islands, separated by the 20–40-mile-wide New Georgia Sound, known as "The Slot" to US servicemen, stretching southeastward from the Bismarck Archipelago over a distance of some 900 miles. The islands cover an area of some 240,000 square miles. The northeast chain includes the main islands of Bougainville, Choiseul, Santa Isabel, Florida, and Malaita. These were of little military value, lacking suitable airfield sites and natural harbors, although Florida was an exception with regard to the latter. The southwest chain includes the main islands and large island groups of the Shortland Islands, Treasury Islands, New Georgia Group, the Russell Islands, Guadalcanal, and San Cristobal.

The islands are of volcanic origin, and were covered by heavily forested mountains. Many of the coastlines were edged with narrow plains. Numerous streams and rivers coursed across the plains from the mountains. In some areas ridges and streams perpendicular to the coast cross-compartmented the plains, presenting ground forces with line after line of obstacles and defendable terrain features. In some coastal areas marshes and mangrove swamps could be found. In other areas dense vegetation grew to the water's edge. Coastal roads were found only in cultivated areas, and native tracks along the shore and inland were rare. Low hills and ridges were common in many coastal areas, rising further towards the interior. These generally had forested slopes with their crests covered by high grass. The climate was harsh, rainy, hot, and humid. Tropical diseases were rampant.

Because of their large size (Guadalcanal, for example, measures 34 by 80 miles), the lack of fringing coral reefs, and the long expanses of beaches they contained, these islands could not be defended from an Allied landing. Indeed, there were few instances of "defense at the water's edge." The Japanese established military bases, naval bases, and airfields and defended these key positions instead, expending little effort to defend the entire coastline. However,

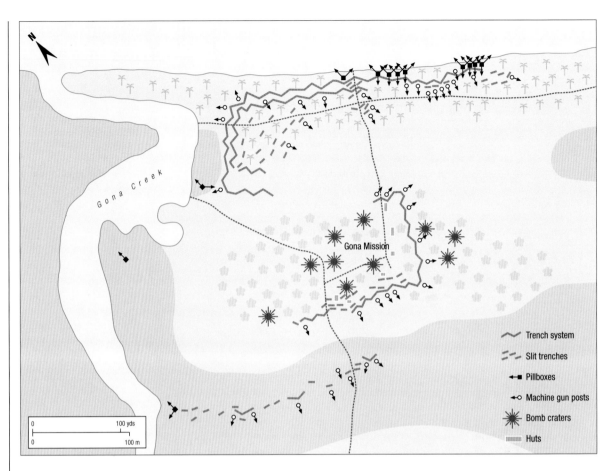

The map legend:
- Trench system
- Slit trenches
- Pillboxes
- Machine gun posts
- Bomb craters
- Huts

Gona Creek

Gona Mission

0 — 100 yds
0 — 100 m

The Japanese defenses at Gona, Papua, November–December 1942, which formed the western anchor of the Gona-Buna beach strongholds. The defense in depth provides three lines of defense, beach defenses protecting the rear, and flank defenses. There are also hundreds of foxholes and dugouts, which are not shown at this scale.

lookouts were posted and coastlines were patrolled by aircraft and small vessels. An Allied landing on the island would be defeated by maneuver. This would be a difficult task because of the non-existent or crude road and trail system. Heavy equipment, artillery, and large quantities of munitions and supplies would for the most part be delivered by barge, and rarely by overland movement.

Three of the major American landings in the Solomons—Guadalcanal, Bougainville and New Britain—saw the establishment of lodgments in which airfields were constructed. US forces would land either unopposed or weakly opposed, and establish a beachhead. As airfields were constructed or captured Japanese airfields repaired and expanded, the Americans established a strong perimeter with ample defenses facing seaward, to protect against counter-landings. Supplies and munitions were stockpiled and patrols sent out to locate and harass Japanese troops in the vicinity.

The Japanese would send forces from their main positions to overrun the lodgment. In the case of Guadalcanal, on which no other Japanese forces were located, they had to be shipped from elsewhere and kept supplied, making the counteroffensive extremely difficult to support. Only on Bougainville was a counterlanding attempted, and it was less than successful. At this early stage of the war the IJA and IJN both had significant airpower in the Solomons, and air attacks on the American beachheads and invasion fleet were frequent. This forced American ships to remain in the area only briefly and to keep their distance; sometimes, this made resupply and reinforcement an erratic process.

Japanese counterattacks would be launched as soon as units could be assembled in the area. Any elements remaining in the area after the Americans had landed were expected to harass the beachhead. When they attacked they often struck the flanks with a main attack and one or two supporting attacks,

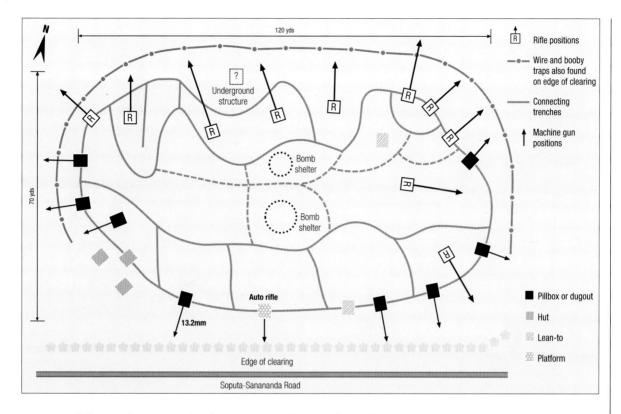

N

120 yds

70 yds

? Underground structure

R Rifle positions

Wire and booby traps also found on edge of clearing

Connecting trenches

Machine gun positions

Bomb shelter

Bomb shelter

Auto rifle

13.2mm

Edge of clearing

Soputa-Sanananda Road

Pillbox or dugout

Hut

Lean-to

Platform

a variant of the enveloping attack. The Japanese made several mistakes during their efforts to overrun the lodgments. They often failed to build up sufficient stocks of ammunition and supplies, being hampered by transportation difficulties and Allied interdiction. The attacks were usually launched without adequate (if any) reconnaissance, and sufficient time was not allowed for units having to cover longer distances to reach their attack positions. There was little coordination between the different attack forces. Artillery support was minimal and the expected air and naval gunfire support was ill-timed or failed to materialize. Units often attacked when they reached their position without waiting for late-arriving units, thus weakening the attack. The resultant piecemeal attacks allowed the defenders to reinforce threatened sectors at will, to reposition their reserves in relation to the relevant sector under attack, and to mass artillery fire on each attack due to the fact that they were launched at different times. More often than not the strength of the defenders was greatly underestimated, often by as much as half of the number of troops actually facing them— with the result that the attack force was insufficient to carry the beachhead. American direct and indirect firepower would devastate the attackers. Even if the attack force had been able to penetrate the perimeter in force, counterattacks and the commitment of reserves would have stopped them. There were many instances of small groups managing to penetrate the perimeter and attack artillery positions, headquarters, and rear area installations, but these were merely of "nuisance" value and of no serious consequence to the integrity of the defense. While Japanese doctrine prescribed flanking and enveloping attacks, in practice reckless frontal attacks were more common with waves of troops charging into devastating fire carrying only their rifles and bayonets.

On Guadalcanal, once the Japanese offensive capability had been broken, the IJA was forced to conduct a fighting withdrawal up the coastal plain, establishing successive defensive lines on the cross-compartmented terrain. Well dug-in defenses were established on hills and ridges and maximum use

This is a simplified diagram of a January 1943 Japanese strongpoint in the Central Sector of South Giruwa, 2¹/₂ miles south of the coast. The Allies designated it "Perimeter Q." The surrounding ground was swampy, and could be up to waist deep after rain.

was made of small caves. As Japanese defensive capabilities crumbled, due to mounting losses caused by combat action and the harsh environment, the lack of supplies, and dwindling air and naval support, the American push to the north drove the Japanese back faster than fallback lines could be prepared for the reeling rear guard. These ridgeline defenses seldom reached further than a half-mile inland.

In the New Georgia Group the Japanese were established in small pockets around the scattered islands. They were defeated piecemeal, though some of the fighting, especially at Munda Point, was brutal. New Britain and Bougainville saw the Marines establishing a Guadalcanal-like lodgment in which airfields were built. The Japanese were battered by the strength of American firepower, and finally withdrew to their own distant end of the island, the Americans being satisfied to harass them with patrols. The relieving Australians later conducted more aggressive, but still small-scale, operations; the Japanese held out until the war's end, having been effectively neutralized by the destruction of their aircraft and barges. There was little sense in the Allies expending lives to destroy such isolated and impotent strongholds.

The US Army and Marine Corps were initially trained for a "conventional" war, one that would employ weapons at long ranges. The jungles and hills initially frustrated their tactics and weapons employment. The Japanese, who were similarly ill prepared due to their combat experience in the open terrain of China and Manchuria, where many of the units covered in this volume served, faced the same difficulties.

Contrary to popular perception, the Japanese were not trained in tropical jungle warfare; they had no suitable location in which to do this. Some units, which had previously fought in the NEI, the Philippines, and elsewhere, were more experienced, but they had taken part in operations that relied on roads. They too had to learn how to deal with the less developed and more rugged terrain found on the South Pacific islands.

The Japanese quickly became adept at jungle warfare, as did the Americans and Australians. They proved to be masterful at camouflage and were extremely effective in concealing pillboxes, trenches, and other positions. Allied troops often only detected Japanese positions when they came under fire at close range.

Table 8: IJA/US unit combat experience comparison

Location	IJA unit	Previous experience	US unit	Previous experience
Guadalcanal	2d Division	Java, Philippines[1]	1st Marine Division	none
	38th Division	China, Hong Kong	2d Marine Division	none
	35th Infantry Brigade	Singapore, Borneo	Americal Division	none
			25th Infantry Division	none
New Georgia	6th Division[1]	China	25th Infantry Division[1]	Guadalcanal
	38th Division[1]	China, Hong Kong, Guadalcanal	37th Infantry Division	none
			43d Infantry Division	none
Bougainville	6th Division	China, New Georgia[1]	3d Marine Division	none
	17th Division[1]	China	37th Infantry Division	New Georgia
			Americal Division	Guadalcanal
New Britain	17th Division	China, Bougainville[1]	1st Marine Division	Guadalcanal
	65th Brigade[1]	China, Philippines	40th Infantry Division	none

Notes: Major IJA and US units fighting in the Solomons and Bismarcks varied in their degree of previous combat experience. Only experience from the past 2–3 years is listed because of troop turnover.
[1] Indicates only elements participated.

They also made effective use of locally available materials for construction and camouflage. Most positions were heavily constructed and resistant to light mortar and artillery fire including the Australian 25-pdr (87mm). US 81mm mortar and 105mm howitzer rounds with delay fusing were required to destroy bunkers; or alternatively, artillery was moved up and fired directly into a position. Defensive positions were known for their depth with multiple positions covering forward positions, the flanks, and rear approaches. The Japanese defense was based on heavy machine guns, which were protected by light machine guns and riflemen. An attack on one position would draw fire from two or more mutually supporting positions. Grenade discharges would cover any approaches. Once the approach of Allied troops had been detected, a high rate of grenade fire would quickly descend on them. Even in small-scale engagements, Allied troops expected to receive grenade discharger fire almost immediately[4].

The Japanese did not necessarily seek terrain on which to establish the defense that permitted long-range fire. Often defensive positions were constructed behind masking terrain features, limiting Allied observation and direct fire. For example, defensive positions might be prepared only 20–50 yards behind a low ridge. This would screen and provide cover to the approaching attackers; the Japanese would post lookouts to warn of their approach and take them under fire with grenade dischargers and mortars as they sought cover behind the ridge. The attackers would be exposed to direct rifle, machine gun, and infantry gun fire when cresting the ridge and descending its rear slope facing the Japanese positions. Often the Japanese would withhold fire until the enemy had closed to within 10 yards. Machine guns would be sighted to fire criss-crossing lines of fire immediately in front of their positions.

The Japanese would establish defenses on jungle-covered hills and ridge masses deep within the jungle. However, this was not for the common reason of obtaining long-range observation and fire; jungle-covered high ground failed to provide this. High ground was usually subject to erosion, was cut by ravines, had rocky outcrops, and offered caves that provided cover and hindered attackers. It was simply harder for the attackers to assault uphill and through dense vegetation.

Positions would often be dug in unlikely locations, such as in a large open field of kunai grass surrounded by forest. The 2–4ft high grass concealed the positions effectively, but attacking troops were exposed. The defenders simply did not concern themselves with the cover and concealment provided by the surrounding forest to the attackers, as they had to expose themselves in order to attack. In other instances a defensive line might be constructed within a forest with a clearing less than 50 yards behind the position. While it denied the defenders covered escape routes, this was not a concern—they had no intention of escaping. However, the clearing to the rear did protect the defenders from a surprise attack from that direction. Natural obstacles, especially swamps, marshes, and open ground, were incorporated into the defense. Little barbed wire was available to the Japanese. It was this ability to make maximum use of the dense and rugged terrain in order to exploit their short-ranged weapons that made Japanese defenses so difficult to overcome.

Snipers were employed extensively, partly to harass and slow advancing Allied troops, but primarily to warn of their approach. Snipers would be positioned to cover approach routes, forward positions, and unit flanks. While snipers occasionally positioned themselves in trees, it was more common for them to be concealed at ground level. The crack of bullets passing over the heads of Allied soldiers gave the impression that the fire was originating from high in trees. Even the Japanese were fooled by this and thought Allied snipers routinely fired from treetops, which was rare. When snipers did position themselves in trees they sometimes tied themselves in. It was assumed by Allied soldiers this

4 See Rottman, G. Fortress 1: Japanese Pacific Island Defenses 1941–45 (Osprey Publishing, Oxford, 2002).

was to make it difficult to determine if the sniper had been hit by counterfire. While this was certainly one result, the real reason they tied themselves in was to prevent them falling out if they should slip, fall asleep, or be wounded.

The Japanese excelled at developing imaginative deception and tactical techniques. They would shout and fire weapons from one direction to draw fire and distract Allied soldiers in night positions while the main attack or infiltration attempt approached quietly from another. They would also mimic Allied soldiers, shout common English names, and yell threats in an effort to get soldiers to reveal their positions.

An effective mortar fire deception technique was sometimes used when the Japanese received American mortar fire. They would immediately begin firing a mortar into the forward American position; only a few rounds would be fired at irregular intervals, as it was apparent to the Americans their own rounds were landing on Japanese positions. The American infantrymen in the frontline, when mortar rounds were dropped in their positions and their own mortars were firing on the Japanese, would call for a ceasefire as it was assumed their own short rounds were hitting them. This deception almost always worked, even though it was used frequently, especially if the Japanese and American positions were in close proximity to each other. The Japanese also used over-flying aircraft noise to mask the firing of mortars and grenade dischargers. Mortars make a very distinct "pop" and have a long flight time; troops on the frontline automatically take cover when mortar reports are

The defenses of Gona, 1942, the western end of the 3¹/₂ mile-long Gona position in the Buna–Gona area. The areas within this position called the Triangle, Coconut Grove, and the Island were particularly difficult to overwhelm for US forces. The defenses also featured hundreds of foxholes, dugouts, and other small positions, which are not shown here. In the upper right are trench lines positioned perpendicular to the coast. These trenches faced Allied troops that had penetrated the outer defenses and were attempting to roll up the defenses from the flank. They proved particularly difficult to take.

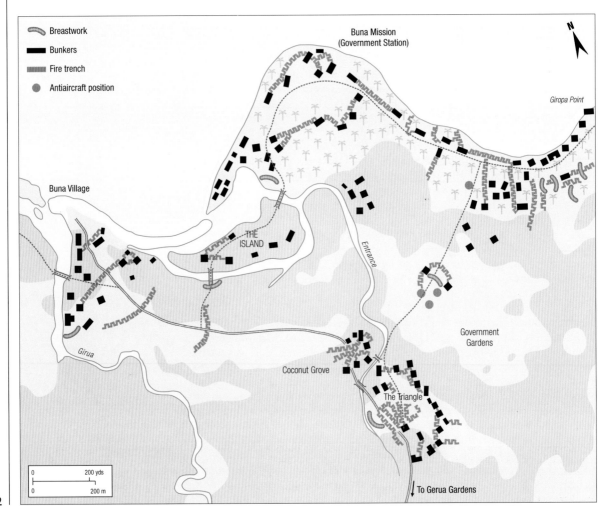

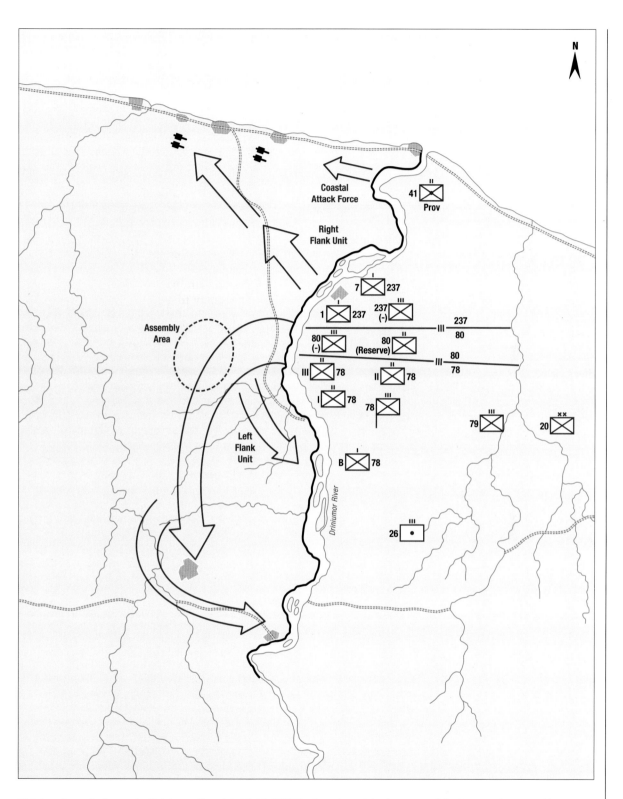

N

Coastal
Attack Force

Right
Flank Unit

Assembly
Area

Left
Flank
Unit

41 Prov

7 237

1 237   237 (-)

237
80

80 (-)   80 (Reserve)

80
78

78   78

78   78

79   20

B 78

Driniumor River

26

18th Army's attack plan on the Driniumor River, July 10–11, 1944. The frontal attack in the center of the American line east of Apitape strove to achieve a breakthrough; it was successful, and created a gap in the line. The 237th Infantry swung north and took up positions behind the US frontline; it remained there for several days, before being driven back. The 78th and 80th moved south to occupy the southern end of the line. US counterattacks were able to restore the line, and had driven the remnants of the 20th Division across the river by August 1.

heard. Passing aircraft would mask the firing signature and exposed troops would be taken by surprise when the rounds impacted.

The Japanese sometimes used pairs of heavy machine guns to fire on a target identified by frontline troops, both by day and at night. Mortar forward observers, to whom the target may not have been visible, would then adjust mortar fire on the point where the machine gun tracer streams crossed.

The Japanese were notorious for their deceptive and often treacherous practices. Playing dead in order to shoot or throw a grenade at passing Allied troops was common. Infiltrators might cut behind-the-lines telephone wires and ambush repair crews. Booby traps were not as widely employed as had been expected. Those used were often easily detected and placed without much imagination or thought. Landmines saw very little use at this stage of the war.

The Japanese quickly became known for their tenacity and willingness to engage in hand-to-hand combat. In the attack they would infiltrate through closely spaced positions, and attack with bayonets, knives, or their bare hands. They would swarm around Allied tanks throwing grenades and launching hand mines. Allied soldiers fighting their way into defensive complexes expected immediate hand-to-hand counterattacks from the defenders.

Japanese armor was employed on a very small scale in the South Pacific. When tanks were employed it was often only two or three at a time, and they were easily knocked out having had little or no impact. On many islands the Allies encountered no tanks. Besides limited sea transportation capability, the main reason tanks saw little use in the South Pacific were the severe limitations imposed by the terrain. The largest Japanese tank action occurred on Guadalcanal in October 1943; all nine attacking tanks were destroyed within minutes.

Japanese antitank defense capabilities were limited yet relatively effective, since the Allies at this stage of the war employed only 37mm-gun-armed light tanks. Heavier M4 Sherman 75mm-gun-armed tanks were not employed in the Solomons or on New Guinea. Light tanks were vulnerable to the modest 3.7cm antitank gun and 2cm antitank rifle as well as determined close assaults by infantrymen. Allied tanks were also hampered by the dense and rugged terrain, being easily mired in mud and swamps, blocked by unseen gullies, and grounded by tree stumps. The thick vegetation also allowed attackers to move in close to tanks unseen. It was essential that infantry accompany tanks in order to protect them. The 37mm tank gun proved to have only a limited effect on bunkers[5].

Japanese artillery tactics came in for much criticism by the Allies. With little need for significant artillery support in the past and the preference for the infantry attack, artillery capabilities were poorly developed. They used outdated fire-control and observation techniques, resulting in slow and unresponsive requests for fire. For the most part fire support was pre-planned to support attacks; units rarely could request on-call support. They had to rely on the limited capabilities of their infantry guns and mortars. Because of the small numbers of artillery employed and cumbersome fire-control procedures, artillery support was weak when attacking on a wide front. The artillery's short range required it be positioned well forward, exposing it to the danger of being overrun by Allied attacks and placing it within range of even light Allied artillery. Delaying positions, such as those used on Guadalcanal, had to be close together because of the artillery's short range. Artillery was registered during daylight for night firing and this sometimes allowed the Allies to shift positions after darkness fell, thus negating the artillery fire. Regardless of the limitations of Japanese artillery equipment and the poor techniques, the major problems facing the artillery were the insufficient ammunition supplies, the great difficulty in moving artillery on rugged tropical islands, and the Allies' massive counterbattery and air attack capabilities.

5 See Rottman, G., Elite 124: *World War II Infantry Anti-Tank Tactics* (Osprey Publishing, Oxford, 2005).

Weapons and equipment

Japanese individual and light infantry crew-served weapons were rugged and mostly reliable, but had comparatively short ranges. Since their weapons were designed to be broken down for mule transport, something wholly impractical in the Pacific Theater, they could be man-packed. However, the latter limited the number of weapons which could be brought forward, and took a terrible toll on the troops. Some equipment designed for tropical use began to be issued at this time and a small number of new weapons were fielded. For the most part, though, the new weapons were only minor improvements over earlier designs, and were inadequate when compared to Western counterparts. Although Japan was allied with Germany, she received little in the way of arms technology, less so than is sometimes speculated.

Table 9: Japanese weapons terminology	
Pistol	Kenju
Rifle	Shoju
Rifle grenade launcher	Tekidanju
Hand grenade	Shuryudan
Light machine gun	Keikikanju
Heavy machine gun	Kikanju
Machine cannon	Kikanho
Automatic gun	Jidoho
Grenade discharger	Tekidanto
Trench mortar	Kugekiho
Regimental infantry gun	Rentaiho
Battalion infantry gun	Daitaiho
Antitank gun	Sokushaho
Antiaircraft artillery	Koshaho
Antiaircraft machine cannon	Kosha kikanho
10cm howitzer	Juryu
10cm gun	Juka
15cm howitzer	Jugoryu
7.5cm mountain gun	Sampo
Tank	Sensha
Tankette	Keisensha
Light tank	Chusensha
Medium tank	Jusensha
Armored car	Sokosha

A light Caterpillar-type dozer tractor bearing the IJN chrysanthemum and anchor insignia, being driven by a US Navy Seabee. The 5-gallon fuel can over the fender is US issue. The Japanese had no equivalent to the "Jerry can," using only 200-litre (approximately 55-gal) fuel drums.

Infantry weapons

The Arisaka 6.5mm Meiji Type 38 (1905) and 7.7mm Type 99 (1939) were the standard rifles. The Type 99 was issued in two lengths, the long infantry rifle being 6in. longer than the short rifle, which was originally intended for cavalrymen, engineers, and artillerymen. Only a few thousand long rifles were produced and by 1940 it was decided to issue only the short rifle to all troops; the long rifles remained in service though. The Japanese had the foresight to produce the Type 99 with a chrome-plated bore to prolong barrel life, ease cleaning, and protect it from tropical rust. A sniper version of the Type 99 short rifle was issued in 1942 fitted with either a 2.5x or 4x telescope. It did not receive a different designation, unlike the Type 97 (1937) sniper version of the 6.5mm Type 38. The Japanese used an effective flashless and smokeless propellant making it difficult for Allied troops to locate firing positions in the jungle.

The Nambu 6.5mm Type 96 (1936) and 7.7mm Type 99 (1939) LMGs were supplemented by the obsolete Nambu 6.5mm Type 11 (1922) LMG. The Nambu 6.5mm Type 3 (1914) or 7.7mm Type 92 (1932) HMGs were supplemented by the new Nambu 7.7mm Type 1 (1941). It was considerably lighter and of more simplified construction than the Type 92. The Nambu Type 14 (1925) pistol remained in production through the war alongside the lower cost Type 94 (1934). The 8mm[6] Type 100 (1940) submachine gun, with a 30-round magazine, saw very limited service. The 5cm Type 89 (1929) heavy grenade discharger was very widely used, and became known as the "knee mortar" to American troops on Guadalcanal.

IJA divisions were mostly armed with either 6.5mm or 7.7mm rifles. However, ad hoc South Seas detachments, garrison units, and replacement units were sent to the South with their battalions drawn from different divisions in Japan, Manchuria, China, and Korea. These different battalions could be armed with different caliber weapons. Both weapons had distinct advantages appreciated by the Japanese soldier, resulting in mixed weapons within IMBs. The 6.5mm had little recoil, but lacked penetration and knockdown power. The 7.7mm, while an awkward weapon, was designed to improve range and power on the Chinese and Manchurian plains and offered effective penetration through dense tropical vegetation.

The Type 2 (1942) rifle grenade launcher was a modified copy of the German cup-type discharger, for which the Germans furnished plans. It was used on both 6.5mm and 7.7mm rifles. First employed on Bougainville, it had a 3cm rifled bore, and fired full-caliber 3cm and over-caliber 4cm Type 2 shaped-charge antitank grenades. At Buna, New Guinea the Japanese made extensive use of spigot-type grenade launchers and even though they fired only the small Type 91 (1931) hand grenade with a finned adapter tail boom, the Americans felt they were extremely effective and at the time had no equivalent.

Type 1 toxic gas grenades were captured on Guadalcanal in 1942, but they were never used against Allied troops other than during a single incident against British tanks in Burma. Intended for use against tanks and pillboxes, they were not very effective. The Type 1 was a small ceramic sphere filled with hydrocyanic acid, a blood gas derived from hydrogen cyanide; the sphere shattered on impact to dispense the small quality of gas. The Type 99 (1939) hand grenade, with an improved fuse for better performance in North China's cold climate, was first discovered by US forces on Kiska Island in the Aleutians

---

6 The 8mm was the same round as that used in Japanese pistols.

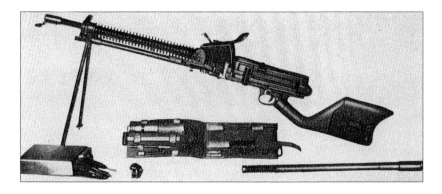

The obsolete Nambu 6.5mm Type II (1922) LMG remained in use in some units throughout the war. Large-scale replacement by the Nambu 6.5mm Type 96 (1936) and 7.7mm Type 99 (1939) did not begin until the end of 1941. The first units to receive these new weapons were elements of the 25th Army in Malaya.

The heavy 2cm Type 97 (1937) antitank rifle saw only limited use, predominantly because it was expensive. This one is fitted with its shield and carrying handles. The shield was often removed to reduce its 150 lb. weight. The handles were generally removed for firing, though it could be fired with the handles in place.

in 1943, and thereafter was commonly called the "Kiska grenade." It could also be launched from the cup-type Type 100 (1940) grenade launcher.

In late 1942 the 4.7cm Type 1 (1941) antitank gun began to be fielded. It was first encountered on New Georgia in July 1943. Large numbers were not recorded by US tank crews until the summer of 1944. The 3.7cm Type 97 or Type Ra antitank gun remains something of a mystery. Six of these weapons were deployed to Guadalcanal with the 8th Independent Antitank Company and were not seen elsewhere, although some were reportedly found at Rabaul after the surrender. This was a German 3.7cm Pak.35/36 and variously reported to have been German-made, captured from the Chinese, license-built by the Chinese, license-built by the Japanese, or purchased from Germany by Japan. The latter is believed to be the case. It is known these guns were test fired against US M3 light tank hulks in the Philippines while 8th Independent Antitank Company was en route to Guadalcanal. The obsolete and inadequate 3.7cm Type 94 (1934) rapid-fire infantry gun served as the primary "antitank" gun. However, an "improved" version, the Type 1 (1941) with a 1.85m barrel (as opposed to the Type 94's 1.7065m barrel) saw limited use. This resulted in only 4mm more penetration at 500m.

Flamethrowers, operated by engineer troops, saw widespread use during the initial conquests and were still encountered in this period even though the Japanese had begun moving to the defensive. The types 93 (1933) and 100 (1940) used two identical fuel tanks holding 2.8-gal and a smaller compressed-air tank. They could fire a 10–12-second continuous burst, but were usually fired in short bursts to 25–30 yards; they had a limited range as they did not use thickened fuel. The difference between the two was a shorter, lighter flame gun on the Type 100. The filled weight of the Type 93 was 55 lb.—the Type 100 was 1.5 lb. lighter.

A US soldier on Bougainville displays a 3cm Type 2 (1942) grenade launcher with a 4cm over-caliber shaped-charge grenade. There was also a 3cm version of this antitank grenade. The rifle is an Arisaka 6.5mm Meiji Type 38 (1905).

Artillery

Divisional and brigade artillery were generally light. Usually there were three battalions of 7.5cm field guns or mountain guns assigned to a division and a small battalion-sized unit assigned to IMBs. A small number of divisional field artillery regiments had a 10cm howitzer battalion; in these cases, it would become the third battalion. The intent was to keep divisional artillery light and mobile and reinforce it when necessary with heavier non-divisional artillery. Heavy artillery was mostly kept under army control for counterbattery and siege work. Most Japanese heavy artillery pieces were obsolescent or obsolete, with the majority of designs dating from World War I and earlier. Some calibers were available in newer models, but older models remained in use due to shortages and limited production capabilities. Range, rates of fire, and projectile effectiveness did not compare favorably to similar Allied weapons. Only 600 artillery pieces over 10cm were produced from 1941 to 1945, along with 6,500 smaller caliber pieces, including infantry guns.

Ammunition for 7.5cm, 10cm, and 15cm pieces usually included high-explosive, shrapnel, armor-piercing, incendiary, smoke, and chemical rounds. Parachute illumination rounds were available in 7.5cm and 10cm. The Japanese believed in light HE projectiles with thin walls. This allowed for a larger explosive charge and longer range, but the resulting fewer and smaller fragments were less destructive to *matériel*. Shrapnel—timed airburst projectiles filled with lead balls—was little used. Incendiary rounds were filled with bursting white phosphorus, carbon disulfide, and rubber pellets; smoke was a burning-type white compound, and chemical rounds were filled with either vomiting or blister gas, which were not used against the Western Allies.

Heavy artillery and even lighter divisional artillery were little used on most of the South Pacific islands and New Guinea. The heaviest use was seen on Guadalcanal and this was limited. Fewer than 50 artillery pieces of all calibers were deployed to Guadalcanal, mostly to support the October offensive. Sixteen 15cm howitzers were deployed; all others were lighter. A comparatively larger number of heavy artillery pieces was employed earlier in the Philippines and Southeast Asia.

Besides the standard 7.5cm Type 94 (1934) mountain gun, mountain artillery units were also equipped with Swedish-made Bofors 7.5cm m/28 mountain guns captured from China. This was a comparatively modern piece with rubber tires and a number were used on Guadalcanal. A few units had some 7.5cm Type 41 regimental guns, which formerly had been the standard mountain gun, making up for shortages of Type 94s.

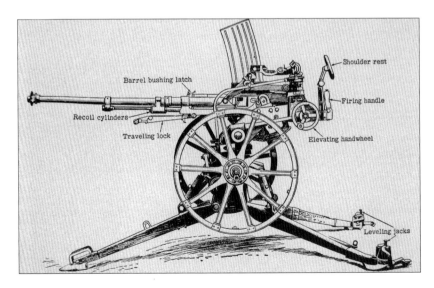

Field machine cannon companies were armed with the 2cm Type 98 (1938) machine cannon. It was intended for antitank, antiaircraft, and antipersonnel use. Its ammunition was not interchangeable with that of the 2cm Type 97 antitank rifle.

While Japan used heavy artillery pieces including 12cm, 15cm, 24cm, and 30.5cm howitzers and 15cm guns, only four 15cm Type 4 (1915) and twelve 15cm Type 96 (1936) howitzers were employed on Guadalcanal. Their ranges were 10,800 and 13,000 yards respectively, while the American 155mm M1918 and M1 howitzers they faced ranged to 12,295 and 16,335 yards respectively. The Type 4 could fire its 80 lb. projectiles at a rate of 3–4 rounds per minute. Ammunition included high-explosive, shrapnel, armor-piercing, smoke, and incendiary rounds. Weighing in at 6,100 lb. it was a difficult weapon to move on Guadalcanal. Its long trails separated in the middle and the rear sections were mounted on a limber with the dismounted barrel while the carriage, cradle, and forward trail sections were moved separately. The two loads required six horses or significant manpower, to say nothing of moving ammunition and related equipment. The Type 96 was considered one of the more modern Japanese artillery pieces. At 8,765 lb. it was even heavier than the Type 4, but could be towed by a truck or tractor without breaking it down into two loads. One of its advantages was that it had a 75-degree elevation, but a deep pit had to be dug beneath the breech to allow for recoil or it could not be fired at an elevation greater than 45 degrees. Another improvement was its 6–8 rounds per minute rate of fire. It used the same ammunition as the Type 4, but a new, slightly lighter, longer-range round was developed.

The 7.5cm Type 94 (1934) mountain gun was widely used in the Pacific in both divisional and non-divisional artillery units. Although obsolete when compared to Allied weapons, its portable nature made it a useful weapon.

Only four 10cm Type 92 (1932) guns were deployed to Guadalcanal, but their long-range fire proved to be a nuisance to the Americans on Henderson Field and were collectively dubbed "Pistol Petes." The Type 92 weighed 6,600 lb. and could be drawn by a heavy truck or tractor. The heavy artillery pieces employed on Guadalcanal were positioned by hand. The rounds, which were actually 105mm, weighed 33 lb. and were available in the same types as the 15cm, but there was also a long, pointed, high-explosive projectile with a 20,100 yard range. The standard high-explosive round had a 16,400-yard range. Its rate of fire was 6–8 rounds per minute.

The 10cm Type 92 (1932) field gun armed Type D medium artillery regiments. To the US Marines on Guadalcanal they were known as "Pistol Petes," due to their long-range, harassing fire.

Antiaircraft guns

The Japanese initially placed only limited emphasis on air defense, and antiaircraft weapons were of outdated design with most having been developed in the 1920s. In theory, the IJA relied on the Air Service to protect ground forces from air attack. Overwhelming Allied air power negated this though, and by late 1943 it was realized that improved antiaircraft weapons, detectors, and fire control were necessary. These measures began to be implemented in early 1944.

Rifles and HMGs were provided with antiaircraft sights, and the latter with AA mount adapters. For large-caliber guns, older methods of fire control were employed in which gun pointers using 2m optical height and range finders, manual target-speed and course-correction calculators, and tripod-mounted 15x binoculars, relayed directions to gun crews verbally. Trumpet-type sound locators, relatively ineffective against modern high-speed aircraft, and searchlights (60, 90, 98, 100, 110, and 150cm) were employed. The tripod-mounted searchlight comparator was a short telescopic device with the operator keeping the targeted aircraft in its crosshairs, automatically directing the searchlight to the aircraft. The cable fitting allowed it to be used with US searchlights. There were no radar-controlled or electronic firing data transfer means. The few crude Japanese radar sets available served only as early warning for the approach of aircraft and sea surface targets. Japanese radar development lagged behind that of the Allies, and was short ranged. Even with radar present Allied aircraft often arrived over the target before effective countermeasures could be undertaken. Wide use was made of observers positioned on high terrain around Japanese-held areas. They were also placed on islands on air routes between Japanese and Allied-held islands and even near Allied airfields, to report incoming air attacks by radio. All Japanese AA weapons were dual purpose and could be used against ground targets.

Field machine cannon companies were equipped with 2cm Type 98 (1938) machine cannons and 13.2mm (.52-cal.) Type 93 (1933) machine guns (generally referred to as "13mm" by the Allies). The Type 38 machine cannon was mounted on a two-wheel carriage with an integral tripod, allowing the wheels to be raised to provide 360-degree traverse. Its 20-round, top-mounted, curved magazine reduced its effective rate of fire, especially against aerial targets. In addition to its air defense role, it was employed against ground targets including light tanks and landing craft. Capable of semi- and full-automatic fire, it had a 120-round per minute rate using high-explosive and armor-piercing tracer. The 13.2mm Type 93 saw limited use by machine cannon units. It was a French Hotchkiss design using a top-loaded 30-round curved magazine. Low ground and high AA tripods as well as wheeled carriages were available. The 87 lb. (without mount and magazine) weapon was capable of 450 rounds per minute with ball, armor-piercing, and tracer, but the need to change magazines (and the absence of a belt feed) reduced its effectiveness. It was often used in the ground role and was especially effective as an anti-boat gun against landing craft and amtracs. The IJN made extensive use of single and twin-barrel 13.2mm Type 93s.

The most commonly seen heavy AA gun deployed to the Pacific was the 7.5cm Type 88 (1928), though only about 2,000 of them were produced. This was based on an unremarkable British Vickers design. A truck-drawn 5,830 lb. weapon, it was transported on a two-wheel carriage from which it was dismounted for firing and five outrigger legs extended. Its maximum elevation was 85 degrees and was provided with high-explosive, shrapnel, and incendiary rounds fired at 15 rounds per minute. A small number of 10cm Type 14 (1925) AA guns (actually 105mm) were built, but they too remained in Japan. Several types of IJN AA guns were

A 7.5cm Type 88 (1928) AA gun. Early in the war Allied flyers expressed the unfounded fear that the Type 88 was a variation of the much more effective German 8.8cm Flak, a concern based solely on its "88" designation. Japan did field a limited number of 8.8cm Type 99 (1939) AA guns copied from the earlier German Navy version (and of a very different design to the normal German "88") but these were only deployed in the Home Islands.

encountered ashore, including the 2.5cm Type 96 (1936) twin- and triple-barrel guns. The 4cm Type 91 (1931) single-barrel gun was a Vickers-Armstrong pom-pom-type (2-pdr) purchased from Britain in 1931. Japan also produced a twin-barrel copy.

Mortars

Japanese mortars were assigned to non-divisional infantry (8cm) and artillery (9cm and 15cm) mortar units, in contrast to Western practice which assigned them to infantry units. This is somewhat surprising as the mortar fulfilled Japanese infantry requirements, being simple to operate, compact, easy to break down into man- or horse-packed loads, and could provide heavy, short-ranged firepower. The Japanese referred to infantry-type mortars as "trench mortars." The 8cm Type 97 (1937) was of the usual Stokes-Brandt design and similar to the US 81mm M1 and Commonwealth 3in. (which was actually 81mm, not 76mm). Ammunition was interchangeable between the US and Japanese mortars and the Japanese commonly used captured US rounds. The Type 99 (1939) light trench mortar was a limited issue short-barrel version. The 9cm Types 94 (1934) and 97 (1937) heavy mortars were originally intended as smoke and chemical mortars. The Type 94 was of unconventional design, but the Type 97 was a Stokes-Brandt design. Their HE rounds were much feared by Allied troops, weighing over three times what the 8cm HE did. The massive 15cm Type 93 (1933) was also of the Stokes-Brandt design, but the Type 96 (1936) was a little seen model with a massive recoil system. There was a short-barrel version of the Type 97, but it was rarely to be found. The 15cm mortars saw some use in the Philippines and Southeast Asia in 1941–42, but were not again encountered by the Allies until 1944.

Engineer units breached barbed-wire entanglements using a small mortar of unconventional design. The 5cm Type 98 (1938) had a steel base to which the limited traverse bipod was fitted with a fixed 40-degree elevation. It fired a stick bomb with 7 lb. of picric acid explosive in a box-like warhead to 420m; or alternatively, it could fire a Type 99 (1939) bangalore torpedo fitted with a fin assembly and point-detonating fuse (giving it an 80in. length and 18.74 lb. weight) to 300m.

8cm, 9cm, and 15cm mortars were provided with light and heavy HE rounds fitted with fuses that could be set for instantaneous or delayed detonation. Illumination rounds were not provided and smoke was little used except with the 9cm.

Table 10: IJA mortars				
Caliber/type	**Total weight**	**Barrel length**	**HE weight[1]**	**Range**
5cm Type 98	50 lb.	25.6in.	14.1 stick bomb	455 yards
			18.37 Bangalore	320 yards
8cm Type 97	145 lb.	45.7in.	7.37 lb.	3,060 yards
8cm Type 99	50.8 lb.	21.5in.	7.37 lb.	2,200 yards
9cm Type 94	353 lb.	48in.	24.7 lb.	4,157 yards
9cm Type 97	233 lb.	48in.	24.7 lb.	4,157 yards
15cm Type 93	558 lb.	60in.	44 lb.	2,290 yards
15cm Type 96	1,760 lb.	52.2in.	56.5 lb.	4,360 yards
15cm Type 97[2]	770 lb.	66in.	56.5 lb.	4,650 yards

Notes
[1] Listed weight is for the heavy HE if both light and heavy rounds were available.
[2] Short-barrel version weighed 512.6 lb. and had a 54.9in. barrel with a range of over 3,000 yards.
See also New Vanguard 54: Infantry Mortars of World War II, Osprey Publishing, Oxford, 2003.

Command, control, communications, and intelligence

Command and control

The Japanese did not possess an effective joint service doctrine. Even the IGHQ was subdivided into distinct Army and Navy sections. At all echelons in which IJA and IJN forces operated, a jointly written "Army–Navy Central Agreement" (*Riku Kaigun Chuo Kyotei*) was negotiated specifying their missions, extent of mutual support, and committed forces. This was often brokered by the IGHQ.

The Southern Army answered directly to the IGHQ, as did the Combined Fleet. The Southern Army roughly equated to an Allied theater of operations. It was headquartered in Saigon, Indochina under Gen Count Terauchi Hisaichi to initially oversee the 14th (Philippines), 15th (Burma), 16th (NEI), and 25th (Malaya) armies.

The 17th Army was organized by Southern Army on May 18, 1942 at Davao, Mindanao under LtGen Hyakutake Seikichi (aka Haruyoshi) originally to execute the July/August New Caledonia, Fiji, and Samoa invasions. When these operations were cancelled, the command was moved to Rabaul on July 24 to conduct operations in the Solomons, New Guinea, and the Bismarcks. A parallel IJN command, the 8th Fleet, was established on July 14, formally taking over on July 24 when its commander arrived at Rabaul. Its mission too was changed when it was re-tasked as the Outer South Seas Force to defend the same area as 8th Area Army. The 4th Fleet, which had conducted the initial seizure of bases in this area, was relegated to its original mission of defending the Mandate plus the Gilberts and Wake as the Inner South Seas Force.

A Japanese light staff car abandoned on Guadalcanal. Most vehicles employed by the IJA were modified civilian designs, though some military specific cargo trucks were developed just prior to the war.

Following the American landings on Guadalcanal, on August 7 Adm Yamamoto established an intermediate naval force under the commander of the 11th Air Fleet at Rabaul. The Southeast Area Force was tasked with controlling IJN naval and air elements charged with reclaiming Guadalcanal.

IJN chain-of-command, Southeast Area, August 8, 1942	
Combined Fleet	Adm Yamamoto Isoroku
Southeast Area Force	ViceAdm Tsukahara Nishizo
11th Air Fleet	ViceAdm Tsukahara Nishizo
25th Air Flotilla	RearAdm Yamada Sadatoshi
26th Air Flotilla	ViceAdm Yamagata Seizo
8th Fleet	ViceAdm Mikawa Gunichi
8th Base Force	ViceAdm Kanazawa Masao

LtGen Imamura Hitoshi, an infantry officer first commissioned in 1907, served as the commander of the 8th Area Army on Rabaul when activated in November 1942 until the war's end.

The situation on Guadalcanal deteriorated, and on November 16 IGHQ reorganized the Southern Army. The 8th Area Army was organized as an intermediate command on Rabaul with the commander of 16th Army (Java) taking control. The 18th Army was activated at Rabaul to take over operations on Eastern New Guinea, allowing 17th Army to focus on the Solomons. The 6th Division under 8th Area Army control was on Bougainville. These assignments would take effect from November 26.

8th Area Army November 27, 1942 LtGen Imamura Hitoshi	
17th Army	LtGen Hyakutake Seikichi
2d Division	
38th Division	
Kawaguchi Detachment (35th Infantry Brigade)	
Ichiki Detachment (28th Infantry)	
65th Brigade (less elements)	
9th Artillery Command	
18th Army	LtGen Adachi Hatazo
South Seas Detachment	
21st Independent Mixed Brigade	
6th Division	
6th Air Division[1]	

[1] Absorbed 12th Air Brigade when activated on November 27 at Rabaul under LtGen Itahana Giichi.

Eventually three divisions would be assigned to 18th Army. On December 24 the Southeast Area Fleet was established at Rabaul under ViceAdm Kusaka Jinichi as a parallel command to 8th Area Army; it assumed command of the Southeast Area Force.

To provide increased command and control over expanding operations in the Southern Area, another reorganization was undertaken in November 1943. The 2d Area Army Headquarters was moved from Manchuria to take over operations on New Guinea and Halmahera under Gen Anami Korechika. It was headquartered at Davao, Mindanao and assumed operational command of: 2d Army, transferred from Manchuria and headquartered at Manokwari,

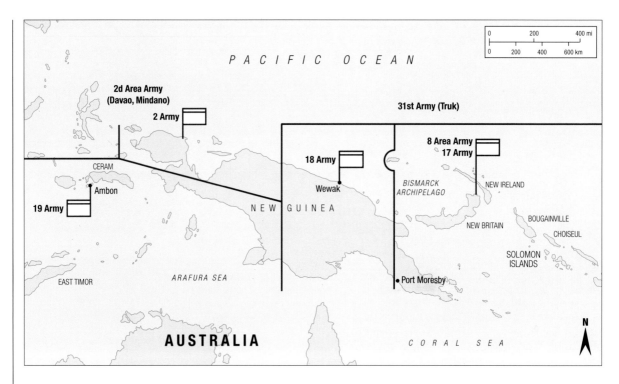

Southeast Area command and control, November 1943.

western Dutch New Guinea under LtGen Teshima Fusatro; 19th Army, headquartered on Amboina Island under LtGen Kitano (aka Kitamura) Kenzo; 4th Air Army, under LtGen Tominaga Kyoji on Celebes; and 1st Field Base Unit[7] on Halmahera. The 4th Southern Expeditionary Fleet[8] supported 2d Area Army. The 2d Army was responsible for Dutch New Guinea and would eventually be assigned the 3d, 35th, and 36th divisions and 2d Field Base Unit, while the 19th Army secured smaller NEI islands south of New Guinea with the 5th, 46th, and 48th divisions. The 4th Air Army possessed only the 7th Air Division on Amboina. The 18th Army on eastern New Guinea was transferred from the 8th to the 2d Area Army at this same time. The 8th Area Army was still responsible for the Northern Solomons and Bismarcks with the 17th Army.

Communications

While the Japanese relied heavily on field telephones and telegraph in China, having only a limited supply of radios, the vast Pacific region with its widely scattered garrisons forced reliance on long-range radio. Field telephones were still extensively used for tactical communications between units, as was telegraph. Tactical radios were also used for inter-unit communications, especially for directing artillery fire and coordinating air support.

Numerous supplementary means of communications were used, including heliograph, semaphore flags, carrier pigeons, and messenger dogs. Japanese aircraft would drop message tubes with colored cloth streamers to ground troops. Colored smoke and pyrotechnic signals were launched from flare pistols, grenade dischargers, and smoke candles. The Japanese would sometimes attempt to deceive Allied troops and airmen by igniting their own colored smoke candles (red, blue, and yellow) whenever Allied troops used colored smoke grenades to mark their positions for aircraft. Allied aircrews soon learned that Japanese smoke colors were not as vivid and dense as their own.

---

7 Field base units were commanded by majors general, and controlled service units; the 1st and 2d were the only such units assigned to Southern Army.
8 Not to be confused with the original 4th Fleet defending the Mandate.

The Japanese Type F collapsible boat was used for landing operations, river crossings, and to transport troops from islands to evacuation destroyers. It could be used singly, but more commonly two 'sections' were fastened end-to-end, allowing 20 men to be carried. One section measured 13 2/3 ft long and 4 3/4 ft wide. Captured boats were routinely used by US troops.

Ground troops would use air–ground signal panels to send simple signals to aircraft and to mark friendly positions. The "T-panel" was essentially a large black cloth square. The regimental number was signaled by positioning two smaller white squares in designated positions and the battalion number by positioning a red triangle in one of three positions. The aircraft confirmed the unit's identification through means of simple, slow messages, achieved by repositioning the white squares in pre-arranged number sequences. The aircraft carried a codebook with these sequences. Panel signaling stations were located some distance from the unit's headquarters.

Protective measures would also be taken for tactical radio transmitters. They likewise would be located a safe distance from headquarters, and moved frequently. Receiver-transmitters would be protected in caves, bunkers, or slit trenches. Orders and information to be transmitted or received would be telephoned to and from the headquarters. Extensive use of messengers would be made in fluid tactical situations. Wire antennae, some 15–20ft long, would

The Daihatsu Type A landing barge was the main ramped landing craft used by the IJA and operated by shipping engineer units. Daihatsu is a contraction of *Dai-Hatsudokitei*— meaning "large motorboat." Each barge was 14.88m in length and had a beam of 3.35m. It could carry 70-plus troops, or 12 tons of cargo, or a medium tank.

In addition to the heavier Model 95 radio transceiver, the Model 92 Revision 3 high-powered set was also used for island-to-island communications.

be strung in trees rather than using more easily detectable pole antennas. The Japanese placed heavy reliance on their codes, confident the Allies would be unable to break them, and seldom changed them. Many of the codes were broken. Codebooks were secured in strongboxes, to which a thermite grenade was attached, but nonetheless many were captured while the Japanese assumed they were all destroyed.

Field telephone lines were usually strung in trees or on poles. Signal units in areas lacking trees carried 1–2in.-diameter, 12–15ft-long poles. They realized artillery could cut aerial lines, but felt they were better protected from vehicle damage and detection by foot patrols. In forward areas though, due to the lack of time, wire was laid on the ground. Wire laying details would make detours and turns when laying wire into headquarters to mislead the enemy. They would also use captured wire laid out as decoys to mislead enemy reconnaissance aircraft. In some areas unfriendly natives cut wire. Because of this, wires cut by shellfire and vehicles, and routine breaks, they would set up wire repair stations to ensure quick restoration of communications.

The Japanese established themselves on numerous widely scattered islands. Distances were vast and communications with higher headquarters required powerful fixed radio stations using Morse code. These stations were protected by heavily constructed, reinforced concrete bunkers with large fixed antenna arrays. When the Allies attacked an island, these installations were usually moved to caves and tunnels, with the original bunkers and antenna towers destroyed. Three models of short-wave radios were employed for this purpose: the Model 95; a 2,200 lb. set; and the Model 95 Mk 4, weighing over 800 lb. As a backup the 450 lb. Model 2 mobile radio was widely used. It could be broken down into horse-packed components, or the components carried on poles for man-packing. When an island was assaulted by the Allies the defenders would transmit their situation, requests for air and sea support, resupply requests, and even lessons learned to higher headquarters. The Japanese managed to keep at least one of these radios in operation until almost the very end on most islands and it was via this means that commanders sent farewell messages.

For news of the war, island garrisons relied on the *Nippon Hoso Kyodai* (Japan Broadcast Network) short-wave broadcasts. NHK and all other news agencies were nationalized by the IJA in November 1941 and all news broadcasts were considered official announcements.

Intelligence

Intelligence was fairly effective in the initial phase of the Pacific War, thanks to several years of aggressive intelligence collection. However, subsequent operations were severally hampered by inadequate intelligence, sometimes no intelligence. The problem was compounded by Japanese staffs constantly making poor estimates of Allied strength, dispositions, and reactions, along with the hope the enemy would act according to the expectations of their often overly complex plans. Aerial reconnaissance played a major role though. At the tactical level, intelligence collection was mainly accomplished through reconnaissance patrols.

Staff intelligence sections at all echelons were looked upon with contempt, being branded as defeatist "nay-sayers," a view often held of logistics staff officers as well. Commanders and operations staff did not want to hear that enemy strength, dispositions, and terrain might not favorably support their plans. Japanese intelligence, prior to World War I, had been a slow, methodical process focusing on regimental level. When war broke out, the focus was shifted to army level, which was concerned with only the broad picture. Offensively minded commanders would rather charge ahead than listen to low-ranking intelligence officers telling them why they should select another course of action. Many intelligence officers were excluded from staff meetings. Operations officers intuitively "knew" anything an intelligence officer could tell them.

Many intelligence officers were relegated to issuing maps, censoring mail, and supervising the code section, which came under the intelligence section rather than signals as in most armies. At regimental and battalion levels, they were known as code and intelligence sections.

The major flaw in Japanese intelligence was cultural prejudice and an attitude created in the IJA that looked disdainfully on the capabilities of foreign armies, real or perceived. The American, Commonwealth, NEI, and Soviet armies were deemed to lack fighting sprit and morale. They were simply not interested in studying them; they felt they were impotent, and suited only for putting down revolts in their colonies; and they felt that they were soft, weak, poorly trained, unmotivated, and cowardly. Such perceptions were reinforced by the poor performance of Chinese warlord armies, where on occasion Japanese regiments defeated two or three understrength, poorly armed, and ill-led divisions. On the other hand their defeats by the Soviets in Manchuria in 1938 and 1939 were glossed over.

The comparatively easy defeats of Western European armies in 1939–41 at the hands of the Germans, the only army Japanese officers respected, validated their contemptuous attitude. The US Army, which had only seen a half-year of combat in World War I, was smaller in 1939 than Switzerland's and Portugal's, and considered amateurish. Very few Japanese officers learned English, preferring Russian, German, or French. Fewer still were assigned to exchange programs or as military attachés to the US or Britain. Those who were found their reports were largely ignored, and they were accused of becoming enamored with the "soft life" and material possessions. Japan also ignored America's natural resources, manpower pool, industrial capabilities, and the extent of Lend-Lease to the British, which began in early 1941.

The comparatively easy initial operations further reinforced the slanted view of enemy armies weakened by the inclusion of native troops. They misread the piecemeal introduction of combat troops to Australia and the South Pacific as lack of will rather than allowing time for training and equipping forces. The US Marine Corps, with three divisions of greater strength and more heavily armed than US Army divisions—certainly more so than Japanese divisions—were viewed as nothing more than small landing units similar to their own Special Naval Landing Forces (SNLF).

After the initial operations, the IJA took a more relaxed attitude, and focused on re-establishing order, administration, and minimal defenses in the occupied areas. Some units were redeployed, returning to Japan or sent to Burma, China, or Manchuria. The Ministry of War felt a mere 21 battalions could secure the Southern Area. The IGHQ rightfully felt a larger garrison was necessary, but itself underestimated the Allies' counteroffensive capabilities. The extent of the Allies' ability to field combat units; build planes, ships, weapons and vehicles; produce supplies and *matériel*; and develop tactical innovations would significantly influence the battlefield, and was drastically underestimated by IGHQ. The 2d Bureau of the Army General Staff failed to foresee the fielding of amphibious tractors and trucks, radar-controlled antiaircraft guns, radar-directed night attack aircraft, large landing craft and ships, and other innovations.

The IGHQ estimated Allied strength on projected objective islands in May 1942 as follows. Japanese estimates were far below the actual strength of the defenders present and the 17th Army forces destined to assault these islands were inadequate.

Area	Estimated strength	Actual strength
Hawaii[1]	35,000 US Army	62,700 US Army
Midway	1,700 US Army and Navy[2]	2,500 USMC
Samoa	750 US Navy	30,000 USMC
Fiji	7,500 US and British[3] Army	10,000 NZ Army, 710 US Army
New Caledonia	3,000 US and French Army	18,000 US Army, 2,800 French, 300 Australian

Notes:
[1] Hawaii, though not an objective, is included to further demonstrate disparities.
[2] "Navy" also includes Marine Corps.
[3] The Japanese did not use the term "Commonwealth," but referred to Commonwealth nations as "British," viewing Australia and New Zealand as British colonies.

Perhaps the most serious intelligence shortfall was the perception that the Allies would not be capable of conducting offensive operations until the end of 1942. This was based largely on the assumption that the Pacific Fleet would not have recovered from Pearl Harbor before that point in time. This led to the Japanese initially committing only minimal forces to the Solomons and New Guinea. The Allied counteroffensive was begun in early August 1942 on Guadalcanal and was soon followed by operations to clear the Buna-Gona area on New Guinea.

Combat operations

This section covers IJA operations from early 1942 into early 1944 conducted in the Solomons and on New Guinea. To the Japanese this region was known as the Southeast Area (*Nanto Homen*). From the Allies' perspective, the Southeast Area was split between two theaters of operation: the South Pacific Area, a subdivision of the Pacific Ocean Area under Admiral Nimitz (southern Solomons and South Pacific islands the Japanese included in their further conquests, but were forced to cancel); and the Southwest Pacific Area under Gen MacArthur (New Guinea, Australia, NEI, and Philippines).

Limited space allows only a cursory study of the many operations executed; however, the initial Guadalcanal actions are discussed in detail, in order to provide a better idea of Japanese tactics. Many operations involved the commitment of additional forces in later phases. The focus will be on detailing the order of battle of the committed Japanese forces and their basic movements, as far as the available information allows.

The IJN (specifically, the 4th Fleet operating out of the Mandate) occupied Rabaul on New Britain and Kevieng on New Ireland in the Bismarcks on March 23, 1942. A key redoubt with army, naval and airbases was established at Rabaul. The neutralization of this bastion would become the primary Allied goal in the region. At the end of March, IJN forces operating from Rabaul secured Bougainville and adjacent islands on the north end of the Solomons. Numerous secondary naval and airbases were established to protect Rabaul. Merely a few weeks earlier, SNLF and II/144th Infantry troops seized Lae-Salamaua on the northeast coast of New Guinea against light Australian resistance. To further secure Rabaul, the Admiralty Islands to the north of New Britain were secured in the first week of April. Barge staging bases were established to support the reinforcement and resupply of New Guinea.

Early May saw the abortive attempt to land the IJA's South Seas Detachment (144th Infantry) and SNLF troops at Port Moresby on Papua's south coast. This effort was defeated when Allied air attacks turned back the invasion convoy during the Battle of the Coral Sea. At the same time (May 4) IJN forces seized Tulagi across from Guadalcanal. This was the British administrative center for the protectorate and had been bombed on 1 May, forcing most Europeans to evacuate. Coastwatchers though began to establish themselves on the islands. On July 22 the Yokoyama Advance Force (elements of the South Seas Detachment) landed at Gona on the southeast tail of Papua in an effort to seize Port Moresby overland. The futile effort lasted to the end of August when IGHQ ordered the advance halted on the harsh Kokoda Trail. By late September determined Australian troops had pushed the Japanese back to the Gona-Buna area to commence an even more brutal fight. Fighting continued in the Lae-Salamaua area. In mid-June the IJN began construction of an airfield on Guadalcanal. It was not discovered by American air reconnaissance until July 4 and was bombed at the end of the month. Fighting continued on New Guinea, with the battle for Buna-Gona lasting into January 1943. In late August SNLF troops attempting to land at Milne Bay on the southeast end of Papua were defeated by the Australians.

The US launched its first World War II offensive and its first significant amphibious operation since 1898 at Guadalcanal. This would began the Allied counteroffensive to clear the Solomons and Bismarcks and encircle Rabaul.

Guadalcanal/Tulagi

Tiny Tulagi Island off the south-central coast of Florida Island was seized by a detachment of the Kure 3d SNLF on May 4. RearAdm Shima Kiyohide oversaw the operation, but he departed on May 10. The 25th Air Flotilla at Rabaul established a seaplane base there. Survey parties reconnoitered Lunga Point on Guadalcanal in May and June determining it suitable for an airfield. This effort was part of the SN Operation reinforcing the Japanese outer perimeter by establishing airfields on Papua and Guadalcanal as well as submarine operations to interdict Allied shipping in the South Pacific. IJN forces on Guadalcanal/Tulagi were under the newly activated 8th Fleet, the Outer South Seas Force, which had taken over from 4th Fleet.

The 1st Marine Division's arrival before dawn on August 7 took the Japanese completely by surprise. US carrier aircraft destroyed the float and seaplanes at anchor off Gavutu-Tanambogo, conjoined islets 2 miles east of Tulagi. The Marines expected some 5,000 Japanese to be present in the area, including a 2,100-man IJA infantry regiment. There were no IJA troops present, only 3,704 IJN personnel, of which 650 were SNLF.

Marine Raiders conducted the first landings on Tulagi at 08.00. This proved to be a vicious fight with determined resistance from SNLF troops in well dug-in positions. Parachute Marines amphibiously assaulted Gavutu at 18.00. The assault units had to be reinforced and Tulagi was secured the next afternoon, with Gavutu-Tanambogo secured the following day. Most of the defenders were killed; 23 were captured, and some 70 escaped to Florida.

The locations and dates of American landings and raids (black), and Japanese reinforcement landings (red), on Guadalcanal, 1942.

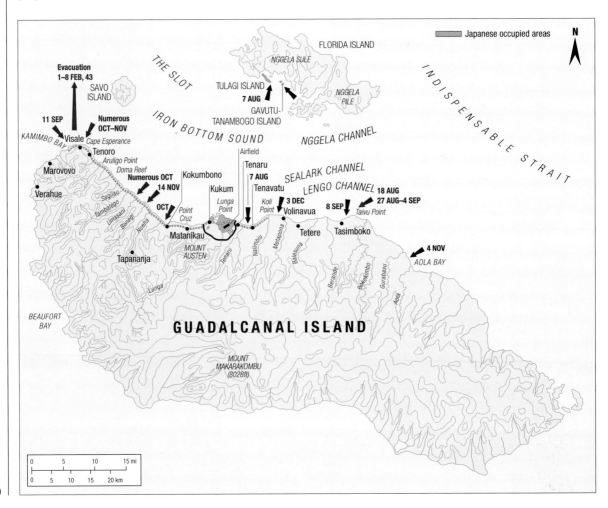

Guadalcanal/Tulagi Defense Force (3,704)	
Gavutu-Tanambogo	
Detachment, Yokohama Air Group (342)	Capt Miyazaki Shigetoshi[1]
Detachment, 14th Construction Unit (144)	
Platoon, Kure 3d SNLF (50)	
Tulagi	
Detachment, Kure 3d SNLF and Tulagi Communications Base (350)	Cdr Suzuki Masaaki
Guadalcanal	
11th Construction Unit (1,350)	Capt Monzen Kanae[2]
12th Construction Unit (1,221)	Cdr Okuma Tokunaga
Detachments, Kure 3d SNLF and 81st Guard Force (247)	Lt Endo Yoshio

[1] Senior officer commanding Guadalcanal/Tulagi Defense Force.
2 Senior officer on Guadalcanal.

Some 23 miles south across The Slot lay Guadalcanal. The main landing occurred at 09.10 about 3¹/₂ miles east of the uncompleted Japanese airfield (*Koku Kichi Gadarukanaru*). The 2,800 construction and SNLF troops were established in two camps north of the airfield and two smaller camps 1¹/₂ miles west. The 10,000 US Marines landed unopposed, and the Japanese fled west. The Marines secured the airfield the next day and began establishing a large perimeter.

IGHQ felt this was only a reconnaissance-in-force and was unconcerned. One result of the American landing was that three transports carrying reinforcements to Buna returned to Rabaul, as their fighter cover was recalled and sent to attack Guadalcanal. Adm Yamamoto assessed the situation differently and established the Southeast Area Force to immediately recover Guadalcanal. The 25th Air Flotilla launched repeated attacks and the 8th Fleet's ships headed south to engage the Americans. This culminated in the Battle of Salvo Island on the night of August 8/9, which the Japanese call the First Battle of the Solomons, costing the Allies four cruisers. The Japanese suffered no losses. With the mounting Japanese air and sea threat, Task Force 61 withdrew that day leaving 10,800 Marines and naval personnel on Guadalcanal and over 6,000 on Tulagi and adjacent islets. They had no air cover, only 20 days' rations, few vehicles, and little construction equipment. The Marine defense concentrated on the flanks and the seaward side to prevent a counterlanding. The densely jungled inland side was only lightly out-posted.

The IJN seaplane base on Tanambogo island north of Guadalcanal after it was attacked by US carrier aircraft, August 7, 1942. Seven 'Mavis' flying boats and eight 'Rufe' floatplanes of the Yokohama Air Group were sunk at anchor just off the photo.

No American reinforcements appeared, which strengthened IGHQ's view that this was a minor operation, with estimated US Marine strength at around 7–8,000 troops. On August 13, IGHQ ordered 17th Army to cooperate with the IJN to recapture Guadalcanal and Tulagi; the Port Moresby landing would be accomplished according to original plans. By late October, 17th Army consisted of the following units.

17th Army, LtGen Hyakutake Harukichi
HQ, 17th Army, MajGen Futami Akisaburo[1] (Chief of Staff)
2d Division
38th Division
21st Independent Mixed Brigade
Kawaguchi Detachment (35th Infantry Brigade)
Ichiki Detachment (28th Infantry)
9th Artillery Command
4th Independent Medium Artillery
10th Independent Mountain Artillery
21st Independent Heavy Artillery (plus companies)
20th Independent Mountain Artillery Battalion
8th Tank Regiment
1st Independent Tank Company
2d, 6th Independent Antitank Battalions
5th, 9th Independent Antitank Companies
3d Trench Mortar Battalion [8cm]
Three Independent Antiaircraft Artillery Battalions
38th, 39th, 41st, 45th, 47th (less elements) Field Antiaircraft Artillery Battalions
37th Independent Field Antiaircraft Artillery Company
19th Independent Engineer (Type A)
4th Independent Engineer Company (Heavy River Crossing)
3d Field Transport Unit
2d Independent Transport Regiment
2d Shipping Transport Group
1st Shipping Transport Unit
1st, 2d, 3d Shipping Engineer Regiments
39th Field Road Construction Unit
Signals Unit, 17th Army
Supply Unit, 17th Army
3d Pursuit Battalion
76th Independent Air Unit (Reconnaissance)
signals, transport, medical, depot, line-of-communications units
[1] *Replaced by MajGen Miyazaki Shu'ichi in September because of his defeatist attitude and ill-health.*

The Aoba Detachment[9], detached from 2d Division and originally destined for Samoa, was assigned to 17th Army; reassigned to 14th Army in July; then back to 17th Army on August 15; and reincorporated into the 2d Division on August 29, the day the 2d Division was assigned to the 17th Army.

9 The detachment was named after Aoba-Jo Castle in Sendai.

The IJN ice plant in the construction base camp near the Guadalcanal airfield. It too was captured by the Marines and made use of. The Japanese sometimes provided more amenable facilities on island bases than is often imagined.

Aoba Detachment, August 15, 1942

HQ, 2d Infantry Group, MajGen Nasu Yumio

4th Infantry, Col Nakaguma

1 Battalion, 2d Field Artillery (Motorized)

4th Company (Tankette), 2d Reconnaissance Regiment

1st Company (added elements), 2d Engineer

Element, Signal Unit, 2d Division

1st Platoon, 3d Company, 2d Transport Regiment

One-third, Medical Unit, 2d Division

2d Field Hospital, 2d Division

Field Water Supply and Purification Unit (less elements), 2d Division

Aoba Detachment, August 1942, Guadalcanal

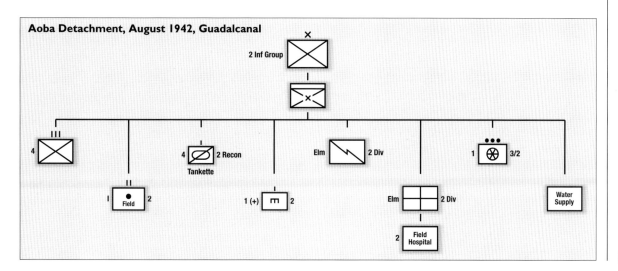

The 35th Infantry Brigade in the Palaus and the Aoba Detachment (both preparing for New Guinea) were available at Davao, Mindanao; however, because it was necessary to exploit the situation before American reinforcements arrived, the IJA General Staff felt smaller units could be deployed faster. The Ichiki Detachment on Truk, placing it much closer than other units, was assigned to 17th Army on August 10 and ordered to prepare along with a detachment of the Yokosuka 5th SNLF. The Ichiki Detachment, built around the 7th Division's 28th Infantry, had originally been the Midway landing force. Sent to Guam when that operation failed, it was returning to Japan when ordered to proceed to Truk and attached to 35th Infantry Brigade. It would be delivered in two echelons. The 35th Brigade would tentatively follow in 10 days. To increase speed, the first echelon was delivered by six destroyers. It departed on August 16 and landed without incident at Taivu Point 20 miles east of the Marine beachhead on the night of the 18/19th. Some 250 SNLF troops landed as a diversion at Kokumbona 9 miles west of the Marines. Henderson Airfield was operational on the 12th and the first of 18 US squadrons arrived on the 21st.

The KA Operation was implemented on August 18 to recapture Guadalcanal/Tulagi. On the 19th Ichiki's advance observation and signal post was virtually wiped out by a Marine patrol, his presence now known about. Ichiki pressed ahead with the aim of bursting through Marine defenses, occupying the former construction unit camp, and then sending out elements to seize the airfield and Lunga Point. Approaching Alligator Creek the force was detected and almost

The Henderson Field attack, and the Battle of Edson's Ridge, September 12–14, 1943.

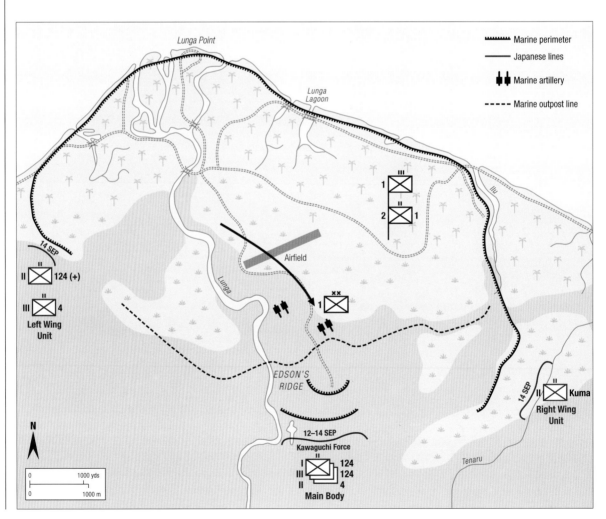

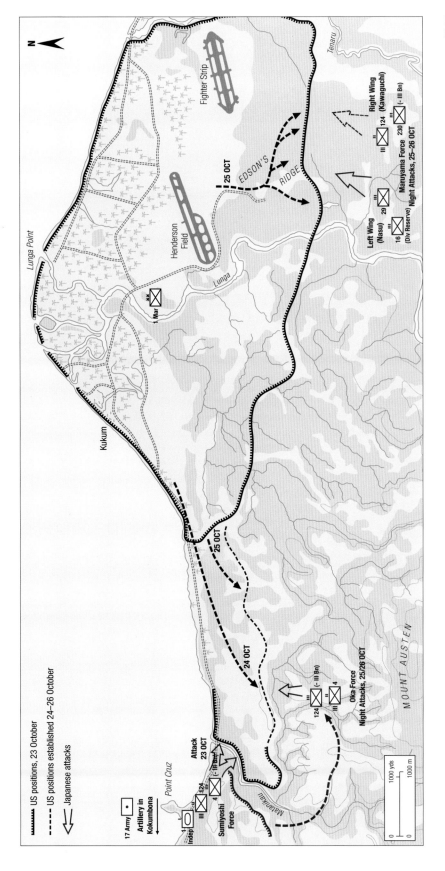

Henderson Field offensive, October 23–26, 1943.

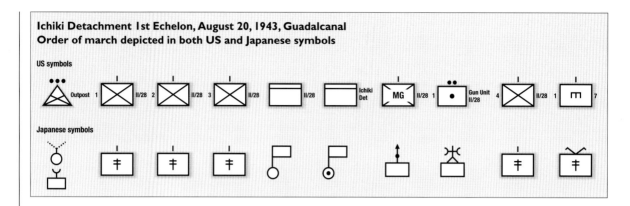

Ichiki Detachment 1st Echelon, August 20, 1943, Guadalcanal
Order of march depicted in both US and Japanese symbols

US symbols

Japanese symbols

Ichiki Detachment 1st Echelon, Col Ichiki Kiyoano (917)
HQ, Ichika Detachment (164)
HQ, II Battalion, 28th Infantry (23)
1st–4th Rifle Companies (420: 105 in each)
Machine Gun Company (110)
Platoon, Infantry Gun Unit (50)
1st Company, 7th Engineer (150)

800 Japanese were killed and 15 captured. Fewer than 130 survivors assembled at Taivu Point. Marine casualties were relatively light.

The extent of the disaster was learned by 17th Army on the 22d, and initially disbelieved, owing to the low esteem in which American troops were held. The Japanese failed to learn from this—and the Americans now understood the Japanese were willing to fight to the death.

On August 16 the Ichiki Detachment's second echelon of 1,100 men (I and III/28 Infantry, 8th Independent Antitank Company) plus 250 SNLF troops departed Truk aboard three transports escorted by a powerful carrier, battleship, and cruiser force. The force's main mission was to engage the American carrier force. The Battle of the Eastern Solomons, or the Second Battle of the Solomons as it is known to the Japanese, ensued on August 24–25; the Guadalcanal reinforcements were forced to turn back after losing a carrier. The transports were attacked and the troops suffered losses.

The Kawaguchi Detachment (35th Infantry Brigade) received 1,000 replacements on Palau in anticipation for commitment to New Guinea. It would be shipped to Guadalcanal aboard transports departing on the 24th; however, the transports were diverted to Rabaul after the Battle of the Eastern Solomons. The brigade would now be delivered by destroyers and barges in the hope that they would be less vulnerable to air attack. On the 26th, II/124 Infantry transferred to destroyers at sea to make the first run, followed by I/124. The destroyer, patrol boat, and barge runs suffered losses, but between August 27 and September 4 much of the brigade and the Ichiki Detachment's second echelon (5,200 troops) landed at Taivu Point. The 1,000 troops transported in 61 barges suffered air attacks and were landed at scattered points, including some 450 of them onto Savo Island. The Ichiki Detachment second-echelon and first-echelon survivors were consolidated into the Kuma (Bear) Battalion. II/4 Infantry was attached from 2d Division.

The aftermath of the September 12–13, 1942 attack on Edson's Ridge south of Henderson Field, Guadalcanal. I/124 and II/4 Infantry of the Kawaguchi Detachment lost some 700 dead and 500 wounded during the battle.

Kawaguchi Detachment, MajGen Kawaguchi Kiyotake (9,700)
HQ, 35th Infantry Brigade (129)
124th Infantry, Col Oka Akinosuka (3,300)
II Battalion, 4th Infantry (658)
Kuma Battalion (former Ichiki Detachment) (1,885)
I Battalion (less 2d Company), 4th Field Artillery (448)
HQ and two companies, 10th Mountain Artillery (442)
Detachment, 20th Independent Mountain Artillery (259)
2d Company, 7th Field Artillery (146)
2d Company, 21st Independent Heavy Artillery (123)
3d Trench Mortar Battalion (404)
HQ, 1st and 2d Companies, 2d Independent Antitank Battalion (123)
Detachment, 6th Independent Antitank Battalion (226)
9th Independent Antitank Company (104)
38th Antiaircraft Artillery Battalion (416)
Detachment, 45th Antiaircraft Artillery Battalion (119)
1st Company, 47th Antiaircraft Artillery Battalion (79)
39th Field Road Construction Unit (247)
Note: All units left rear echelons and some heavy weapons behind because of shipping space limitations.

On September 8 the Kawaguchi Detachment had assembled 6,200 troops, most of them at Taivu Point; however, Col Oka was at Kokumbona Point with his regimental headquarters and II/124 some 30 miles west of the main body. This was not considered a liability though, as the Japanese preferred to attack opposite flanks. On September 2 engineers began cutting a trail from Tasimboko, a few miles west of Taivu Point, to the Marine perimeter. This was extremely hard work due to the ravines, ridges, dense jungle, and streams. The infantry and artillery followed.

The Marine perimeter's flanks and seaward side were well defended, but an 8,000 yard inland sector was manned only by outposts of amphibian tractor, pioneer, and engineer units. A ridge in the center of this sector could provide the Japanese with a direct approach to Henderson Field. The combat-depleted 1st Raider and 1st Parachute Battalions were consolidated and assigned to defend the ridge. The main Japanese attack would punch through the center of the poorly defended inland sector with supporting attacks hitting the inland flanks. Artillery would be positioned to the east of the perimeter. On the 8th

Five of the 1st Independent Tank Company's nine tanks that attempted to cross the mouth of the Matanikau River, Guadalcanal on a sandbar, October 24, 1942. Of the 44 crewmen, 17 survived, of whom seven were wounded.

Kawaguchi Detachment, August–September 1942, Guadalcanal

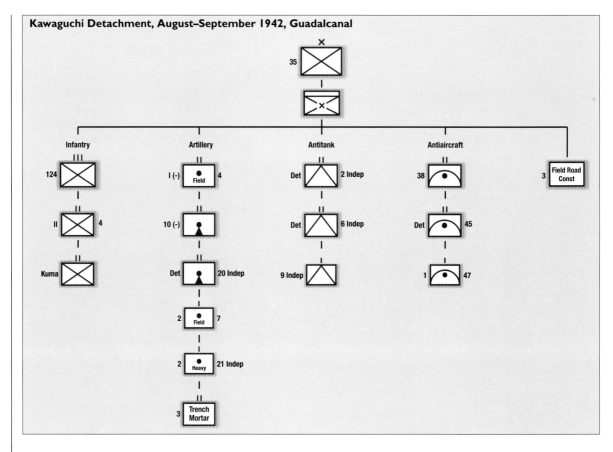

most of the Main Body and Right Wing Unit troops were at Koli Point, five miles from the perimeter, and would begin their approach the next day.

There was confusion between the IJA and IJN as attack dates were changed, and the IJN was told it would be launched on September 11. The attack would be launched on the 12th though. On the night of the 11th III/4 with 630 troops landed at Kamimbo Bay on the island's northwest end. Barges transported them to Point Cruz with many lost to air attack. Col Oka's 650 troops linked up with Capt Monzen and the remaining 1,200 construction and 450 SNLF troops who had fled the Marine landing. The attack was launched on the night of the 12th. The Left Flank Unit was able to attack with only two companies and not two battalions as planned, and did not make it to its assault position in time to contribute. The Right Flank Unit too was in a poor position. The main attack, with 2,500 men, was late launching and units went astray, becoming lost in the jungle resulting in scattered firefights.

Another effort was launched the next night resulting in the destruction of I/124 and II/4 on Edson's Ridge (aka Bloody Ridge); III/124's attack floundered, with few making it to the objective. The flanking units' attacks were again late and impotent. The Kuma Battalion attempted to attack the next night, but the location of the Marine line was unclear and they too were beaten back. The Japanese lost almost 1,000 dead. Large numbers of wounded died as the remnants moved west to Kokumbona, the lead elements arriving there on the 19th. All heavy weapons and half the rifles were abandoned. Marine losses were light.

The 17th Army was stunned at the news. The Americans were not so "soft" after all. The failure was attributed to poor communications and maps, the use of barges to transport troops, widely scattered forces, ration stocks lost to a Marine raid, and American firepower and air superiority. Recognizing the seriousness of the situation, 17th Army ordered significant reinforcement.

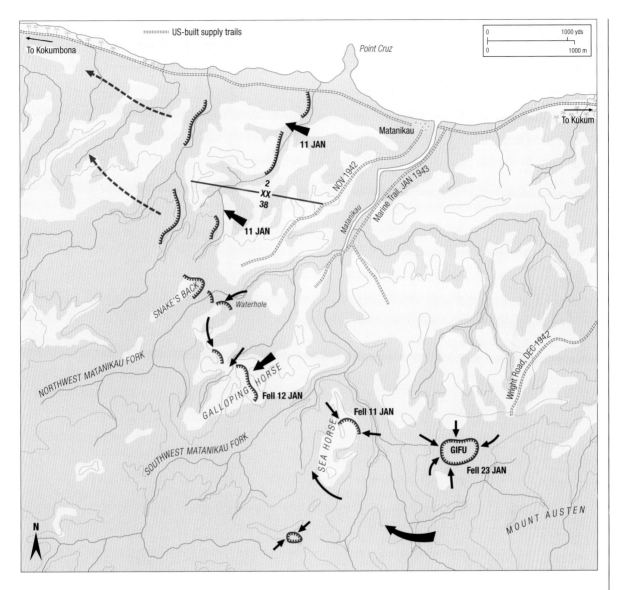

US-built supply trails

To Kokumbona

Point Cruz

To Kukum

Matanikau

11 JAN

2
XX
38

NOV 1942

Matanikau

Marine Trail, JAN 1943

11 JAN

SNAKE'S BACK

Waterhole

NORTHWEST MATANIKAU FORK

GALLOPING HORSE

Fell 12 JAN

SOUTHWEST MATANIKAU FORK

SEA HORSE

Fell 11 JAN

GIFU

Fell 23 JAN

Wright Road, DEC 1942

MOUNT AUSTEN

N

The Japanese line, December 1942—January 1943.

Kawaguchi Detachment, September 8–14, 1942

Main Body, MajGen Kawaguchi Kiyotake

    I Battalion, 124th Infantry Maj Kokusho Yukichi

    III Battalion, 124th Infantry LtCol Watanabe Kusukichi

    II Battalion, 4th Infantry Maj Tamura Masao

Right Wing Unit

    Kuma Battalion Maj Mizuno Eishi

Left Wing Unit

    HQ, 124th Infantry Col Oka Akinosuka

    II Battalion, 124th Infantry Maj Takamatsu Etsuo

    11th & 12th Construction Units &

        Detachment, Kure 3d SNLF, Capt Monzen Kanae

III Battalion, 4th Infantry (support)

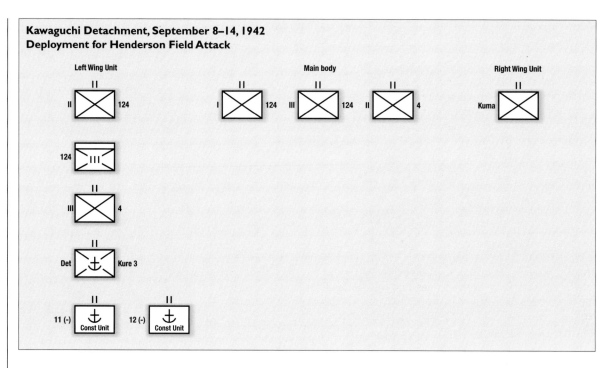

Kawaguchi Detachment, September 8–14, 1942
Deployment for Henderson Field Attack

Left Wing Unit

II | 124

124 | III

III | 4

Det | Kure 3

11 (-) Const Unit   12 (-) Const Unit

Main body

I | 124   III | 124   II | 4

Right Wing Unit

Kuma

All levels of Japanese command now realized Guadalcanal was the focal point of the American counteroffensive. The 2d Division and part of the 38th would be committed and an additional division was requested along with a tank regiment, artillery and signals units, and large numbers of porters. The 38th had been assigned to 17th Army on September 17. Both the IJA and IJN vowed to commit large numbers of aircraft to the KA Operation and an October offensive was planned to drive the Americans into the sea. X-Day was tentatively pencilled in for October 15. The 17th Army staff was increased to cope with expanding operations. It still believed only 7,500 Marines were ashore; in truth, there were 19,000, and by the time of the October offensive there would be 23,000 including reinforcing Army units.

A US Marine logistics trail built by combat engineers as the US offensive pushed northwest from the Henderson Field perimeter. The Japanese lacked the ability to construct such a logistics infrastructure. The open, kunai grass-covered crests are typical of Guadalcanal's hills and ridges.

The IJN committed five transports, 27 destroyers, and two seaplane carriers (for artillery) to deliver units to Guadalcanal via high-speed convoys. Barges would still be used to deliver artillery and supplies, though inadequate staging bases and support were provided. Through late September and early October the Kawaguchi Detachment was engaged in battles around the Matanikau River as the Marines pushed their perimeter westward. It was to secure positions there to cover the reinforcement landings. Air raids on Henderson Field continued and the "Tokyo Express" run of ships down The Slot to bombard the airfield continued intermittently. By the time the 2d Division arrived, 2,000 of the 9,000-man Kawaguchi Detachment were dead, and 5,000 were wounded and ill. The 2d Division was deployed from Rabaul (some elements were in the Shortlands) along with elements of the 38th Division, landing west of the Matanikau River. Some 20,000 troops were assembled by mid-October. 17th Army Headquarters arrived October 9 and situated itself at Kokumbona with 400 17th Army headquarters and signal personnel and a like number of transport and medical personnel. Additionally, over 600 Maizuru 4th SNLF troops were delivered to complement the in-place Yokusaka 5th SNLF troops. The five original 600-man battalions of the Ichiki and Kawaguchi Detachments totaled no more than 700 effectives, and the 4th Infantry's battalions were only about one-third strength. Little artillery remained and a third of the supplies landed were destroyed by air attacks. The 2d and 38th divisions' elements committed to Guadalcanal are listed below.

2d Division (9,847), LtGen Maruyama Masao
HQ, 2d Division (271), Col Tamaoki (Chief of Staff)
HQ, 2d Infantry Group (88), MajGen Nasu Yumio
4th Infantry (2,300)
16th Infantry (2,300)
29th Infantry (2,330)
2d Artillery (less 4th Company and III Battalion) (851)
2d Engineer (664)
2d Transport Regiment (317)
Detachment, Signal Unit, 2d Division (159)
Medical Unit, 2d Division (286)
1st Field Hospital (less elements) (105)
4th Field Hospital (less elements) (78)
1st Independent Tank Company (100)

38th Division (6,696), LtGen Sano Tadayoshi
HQ, 38th Division (89)
HQ, 38th Infantry Group (69), MajGen Ito Takeo
228th Infantry (2,431)
230th Infantry (less 6th, 7th Companies) (2,300)
I Battalion, 229th Infantry (580)
Two companies, 38th Mountain Artillery (250)
38th Transport Regiment (301)
Detachment, Signal Unit, 38th Division (91)
Detachment, Medical Unit, 38th Division (85)

The Japanese attempted to supply its beleaguered forces on Guadalcanal using fast destroyer convoys and submarines. Besides diverting these submarines from anti-shipping offensive operations, they delivered only a small amount of supplies. (Tokushiro Kohayakawa)

Because of delays X-Day was moved to October 22, then to October 24. Two forces would launch the attack. The Maruyama Force (2d Division) would attack in two wings from the south just east of Edson's Ridge to seize the airfields. They departed October 16–18 coping with a grueling trail as they circled south of the Marine perimeter.

Maruyama Force, October 16-24, 1942; LtGen Maruyama Masao
Left Wing Unit, MajGen Nasu Yumio
29th Infantry, Col Furimiya Masajiro (KIA, Col Obara took command)
Right Wing Unit, MajGen Kawaguchi Kiyotaki
230th Infantry (less II Battalion), Col Shoji Toshinari
III Battalion, 124th Infantry
Division Reserve (following Left Wing)
16th Infantry, Col Hiroyasu Toshiro (KIA, Col Sakai Yoshitugu took command)

Elements of the 3d Trench Mortar Battalion, antitank, mountain artillery, and engineer units were attached to both wings.

The Sumiyoshi Force was divided into three elements. The Oka Force would attack from the south at the western extension of the Marine perimeter. The main Sumyoshi Force would attack the extreme coastal west end of the perimeter on the Matanikau River. MajGen Sumiyoshi Tadashi, also 17th Army artillery officer, controlled 15 x 15cm howitzers, 7 x 10cm guns and howitzers, 7 x 7.5cm field guns, and 3 x 7.5cm mountain guns which were positioned at Kokumbona on the coast west of the perimeter. I/228 Infantry and a company of the 38th Engineer (Koli Detachment) would land at Koli Point on X+1 to attack a non-existent US airfield. Because MajGen Kawaguchi kept deviating from orders, he was relieved on October 23 and the Kawaguchi Detachment ceased to exist being absorbed into 2d Division.

The attack was delayed another day, but the order was not received in time. With some units still moving into position, and others in wrong positions, the attack was launched piecemeal. The 1st Independent Tank Company[10] led the assault, attempting to cross the mouth of the Matanikau River; all its tanks were

---

10 1st Independent Tank Company comprised seven Type 97 medium tanks, two Type 95 light tanks. Two other medium tanks were damaged when landing and not committed.

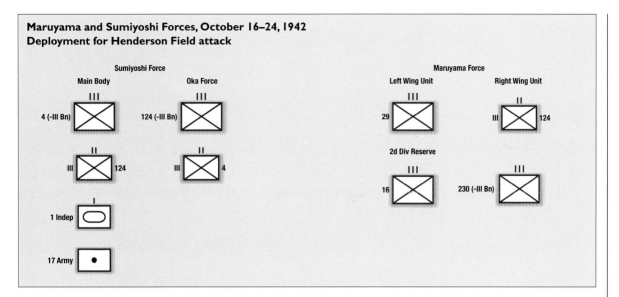

Maruyama and Sumiyoshi Forces, October 16–24, 1942
Deployment for Henderson Field attack

destroyed. The attacks lasted through the night and were pummeled by US air and artillery. Though the IJN shelled and bombed the beachhead relentlessly in the Battle for Henderson Field, it did not help the failed attack, which was beaten back in all sectors. The 29th Infantry made an attack the next night, but this too failed. An estimated 3,000 Japanese died in the October offensive.

From this point the Japanese realized the fight was decisive and regardless of reverses they prepared for another offensive. The rest of the 38th Division was ordered to the island. The 2d Division withdrew to the west, however, and was incapable of offensive action. It is from this point that detailed orders of battle cannot be determined, as shattered units were severally understrength with elements intermingled and sometimes consolidated, and barely able to retain their identity.

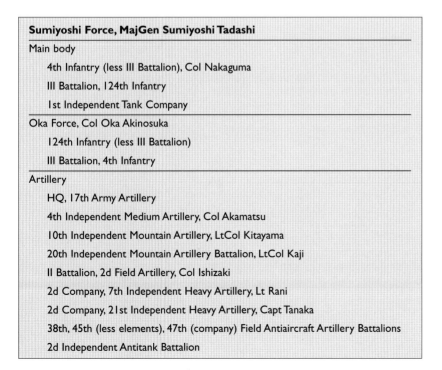

Sumiyoshi Force, MajGen Sumiyoshi Tadashi

Main body

    4th Infantry (less III Battalion), Col Nakaguma

    III Battalion, 124th Infantry

    1st Independent Tank Company

Oka Force, Col Oka Akinosuka

    124th Infantry (less III Battalion)

    III Battalion, 4th Infantry

Artillery

    HQ, 17th Army Artillery

    4th Independent Medium Artillery, Col Akamatsu

    10th Independent Mountain Artillery, LtCol Kitayama

    20th Independent Mountain Artillery Battalion, LtCol Kaji

    II Battalion, 2d Field Artillery, Col Ishizaki

    2d Company, 7th Independent Heavy Artillery, Lt Rani

    2d Company, 21st Independent Heavy Artillery, Capt Tanaka

    38th, 45th (less elements), 47th (company) Field Antiaircraft Artillery Battalions

    2d Independent Antitank Battalion

Reinforcement efforts continued with the 38th Infantry Group Headquarters and 228th Infantry (less II Battalion) led by Col Suemura Masaichi[11] landed on northwest Guadalcanal between 28 October and 8 November. Higher headquarters were dissatisfied with the commitment of the 38th Division, intended for New Guinea, but did promise the 51st Division in China and the 21st MIB[12] in Malaya. Shipping resources were inadequate to deliver these forces, which required almost 900 ship sorties, and would never arrive. An IGHQ officer arrived to assess the situation and reported, "The actual situation is beyond imagination." Regiments were down to a few hundred men; some battalions had fewer than 100 effectives. Some 3,000 Maruyama Force troops west of the perimeter set out east skirting the perimeter. Only 800 rejoined 17th Army.

A major Japanese reinforcement attempt would be made on November 14, Z-Day. This resulted in the Naval Battle of Guadalcanal, November 12–15. Eleven transports would deliver the remaining 10,000 men of the 38th Division, 229th (less III Battalion) and 230th Infantry, and 38th Mountain Artillery. The Japanese lost two battleships, a cruiser, three destroyers, and all transports. Four managed to beach at Tassafaronga, landing 4,000 troops. The 17th Army was now cut off and dug in on a J-shaped line running from the west side of Mt. Austen and circling north to the coast. The 38th Division held the inland line with 2d Division remnants only 1,500 yards from Point Cruz, with fewer than 100 men per "regiment." More US Army reinforcements arrived and there were now 40,000 Americans facing 25,000 exhausted Japanese. Particularly strong Japanese resistance was encountered on three inland ridges: the Gifu (named after a prefecture on Honshu, Japan), Seahorse, and Galloping Horse (named after their shapes). By early January the Mt. Austen area south of the perimeter had mostly been cleared. The Seahorse, held by III/124, fell on January 11 and the Galloping Horse, held by III/228 and 230th Infantry elements, on the 12th. The Gifu, held by remnants of the II/124 and 10th Mountain Artillery, was not taken until the 23rd. Kokumbona was secured on the 25th and the Japanese were in full retreat. The Americans too were exhausted. The Americans received intelligence that up to a division would be landed, but it never materialized.

In early January, IGHQ determined Guadalcanal was untenable and developed plans to evacuate. KE Operation plans, termed a "reinforcement," were completed on January 9, 1943. They expected only one-third of 17th Army to survive and half of the 21 destroyers to be lost. Significant combat ships and air resources would be committed. A specially formed battalion sent to Guadalcanal arriving 14/15 January provided a fresh rear guard for the withdrawal. The Yano Battalion was formed from 750 reservist replacements intended for the 230th Infantry and augmented by a 100-man 7.5cm regimental gun company. Maj Yano Keiji presented LtGen Miyazaki with the withdrawal order. Some officers wished to conduct a *gyokysai* ("breaking of the jewels") final attack, sacrificing themselves, but the withdrawal began on the 20th. The 2d Division was down to 3,700 men.

The 17th Army Headquarters withdrew to Cape Esperance on Guadalcanal's northwest end on January 22 and 38th Division remnants began to disengage. The Yano Battalion was committed at this time to cover the withdrawal of the 2d Division and then fought a series of delaying actions falling back on ridges to defend reverse slopes. While the evacuation force suffered American attacks, for the most part it was successful with 10,652 men recovered on the nights of February 1/2 (4,935), 4/5 (3,921), and 7/8 (1,796) including most of the rear guard supported by a single 15cm howitzer to the end. Only one destroyer was lost. The troops were shipped to the Shortlands and then Rabaul where the

---

11 He was soon killed, and Maj Nishiyama took command.
12 170th Infantry, artillery battalion; tank, antiaircraft, engineer, signals, and transport units; and field hospital.

2d and 38th Divisions were partly rebuilt. Some 31,400 IJA troops and 4,800 IJN personnel served on Guadalcanal. Approximately 11,400 were evacuated, 9,000 died of disease, and 1,000 were taken prisoner.

Guadalcanal losses, August 1942–February 1943		
	Japanese	Allied
Troops ashore (dead)	25,600	1,800
Naval at sea (dead)	3,500	4,900
Aviation (dead)	1,200	420
Ships[1]	38	25
Aircraft	880	615

[1] Does not include small craft.

New Georgia

The New Georgia Group is located 180 miles northwest of Guadalcanal. In the following section, the phrase "New Georgia Group" refers to the group of islands, while "New Georgia" refers to the largest of the 11 main islands covering a 40 by 150 mile area. The islands are hilly, rugged, and covered with dense jungle and underbrush. Slow moving, mangrove-lined rivers flow out of the hills into the sea on the larger islands. New Georgia measures 45 by 35 miles and landing beaches are limited, with the jungle fringing almost the entire cliff-faced coast. Off New Georgia's west end are Kolombangara and Arundal. To the southeast is Vangunu and to the south is Rendova.

The Japanese reconnoitered New Georgia in October 1942 in search of airfields to support the defense of Guadalcanal. In mid-November three Sasebo 6th SNLF companies searched the area for Coastwatchers. Two IJA rifle companies and two antiaircraft battalions arrived at Munda Point on the southwest end of New Georgia on November 20–21, and IJN construction troops landed on the 23rd to build an airfield. In spite of Allied bombing it was completed in mid-December and an airfield was built at Vila on Kolombangara. No air units were based at Munda, as it was used as a re-fueling stop for attacks on Guadalcanal-Tulagi. The Japanese decided New Georgia would be the next major Allied objective.

Between February and May 1943 the Japanese reinforced the New Georgia Sector with a joint IJN/IJA force, the 8th Combined Special Naval Landing Force (CSNLF) under RearAdm Ota Minoru (who commanded the Midway Landing Force transports in May 1942). Yokosuka 7th SNLF (Cmdr Takeda Kashin) arrived on February 23 and garrisoned Kolombangara with 2,000 men including a battalion of the 51st Division. A 6th Division battalion relieved it in April. The Kure 6th SNLF (Cmdr Okumura Saburo) with over 2,000 troops established defenses on New Georgia on March 9 around Munda Point and at Bairoko Harbour and Enogai Inlet. The 229th Infantry, 38th Division reinforced Munda in April. The Japanese expected the Allies to first attack Kolombangara then land north of Munda on New Georgia's upper west coast and attack the airfield to the south. On May 31, the joint forces

MajGen Sasaki Noboru, a cavalry officer, commanded the 38th Infantry Group on New Georgia Island, and put up a strong defense of Munda Point in July and August 1943.

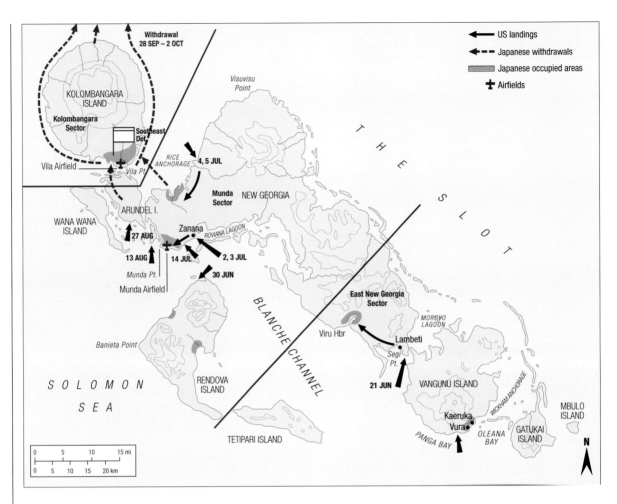

New Georgia Group, June–October 1943

were placed under the commander of the 38th Infantry Group, as the Southeast Detachment (*Nanto Shitai*), and headquartered at Vila. Administratively it was under the 17th Army at Rabaul, but under the operational control of the 8th Fleet. The IJA and IJN units on New Georgia and Kolombangara were reinforced with artillery, antiaircraft, antitank, and engineer units with joint detachments sent to Viru Harbour and Wickham Anchorage on the southeast end of New Georgia and to Rendova Harbour on the north end of Rendova and Kaeruka and Vura Villages on the southeast coast of Vangunu Island. Before the end of the Guadalcanal campaign the IJN established a seaplane base at Rekata Bay on the northeast coast of Santa Isabel to keep The Slot and Guadalcanal under surveillance. Regardless of past IJA and IJN animosities, on New Georgia they operated effectively together.

As Allied aircraft bombed Munda Point, the main American landing was preceded by several small-scale landings on New Georgia, Vangunu, and Rendova to secure anchorages and allow a build up prior to the assault on Munda. The first phase of the operation began on June 21, 1943 when lodgments were secured by Marine and Army elements at Segi Point and Viru Harbour (June 21–July 1) on the southeast end of New Georgia; Wickham Anchorage on the southeast side of Vangunu (June 30–July 3); and Rendova Harbor on the north side of Rendova (June 30). These Japanese outposts were wiped out except for 170 men who escaped from Viru. An emergency US airfield was built at Segi.

The main US 43d Infantry Division landing came ashore on New Georgia in the afternoon of July 2 at Zanana Beach 6 miles east of Munda. The terrain between Zanana Beach and Munda Point is cross-compartmented by streams,

New Georgia Group, June 30, 1943
Southeast Detachment (5,000), MajGen Sasaki Noboru
HQ, 38th Infantry Group, LtCol Kamiya Yashiharu (Chief of Staff)
13th Infantry, 6th Division, Col Hirata Genjiro
I Battalion, Maj Hara Masao
II Battalion, Maj Sato Giichi
III Battalion, Capt Kojima Bunzo
229th Infantry, 38th Division, Col Tomonari Satoshi
I Battalion, Maj Kinoshita Shishu
II Battalion, Maj Ohashi Takeo
III Battalion, Maj Takabayshi Uichi
II Battalion, 10th Independent Mountain Artillery, LtCol Kitayama Masatsuga
2d Independent Antitank Battalion [3.7cm and 4.7cm]
15th Antiaircraft Artillery Group, Col Shiroto Sanichi
8th CSNLF[1] (5,500)
Kure 6th SNLF
Yokosuka 7th SNLF
21st Antiaircraft Unit
17th and 131st Construction Units
Lookout Company, 8th CSNLF
Landing Craft Company, 8th CSNLF
Santa Isabel
7th CSNLF (4,200)
Kure 7th SNLF (3,400)
III Battalion, 23d Infantry, 6th Division (800)
[1] Maisuru 4th SNLF was assigned, but deployed elsewhere.

ridges, ravines, rocky knolls, outcroppings, and tangled jungle. Land navigation was extremely difficult and units could not pinpoint their locations in the chaotic terrain. The fight toward the airfield was agonizingly slow and vicious with seven infantry regiments from the 43d, 37th, and 35th Infantry Divisions sucked into the fight. Five regiments were forced to fight on a 2,000 yard front; on normal terrain a single regiment would advance on a 2,500 yard front. The terrain was so difficult and the Japanese defense so audacious that another landing was conducted closer to Munda on July 14. Munda Point was defended by 229th Infantry (less I and III battalions) and reinforced from Kolombangara by III/229 on July 4 and 13th Infantry; 6th Division in mid-July along with II/10 Independent Mountain Artillery; plus antiaircraft, antitank, engineer, and signals units, followed by II/230 Infantry. At the same time II/45 deployed from Bougainville to Bairoko north of Munda. The Americans finally seized the airfield on August 4 and the surviving Japanese withdrew north with the 13th Infantry covering. The survivors were withdrawn to Kolombangara from August 7, leaving behind 2,500 dead.

In the meantime Marine and Army units landed at Rice Anchorage 16 miles northeast of Munda. They moved southeast six miles to the Dragons Peninsula securing Enogai Inlet and Bairoko Harbour on July 5 to block Japanese reinforcements from the south. This area was defended by some 1,500 men of II/45 Infantry and 8th Company, 6th Field Artillery plus Kure 6th SNLF troops.

East New Georgia Sector
Viru Harbour, New Georgia (230)
4th Company (less platoon), I Battalion, 229th Infantry
Mixed detachment, Kure 6th and Yokosuka 7th SNLF
Infantry gun and antiaircraft gun detachments
Wickham Anchorage, Vangunu (120)
Company, Kure 6th, SNLF
Platoon, 4th Company, I Battalion, 229th Infantry
Munda Sector (aka Central New Georgia Sector)
Munda Defense Unit
HQ, Southeast Detachment
229th Infantry (less 3d and 7th Companies)
II Battalion (less 6th Company), 10th Independent Mountain Artillery
2d Independent Antitank Battalion (less elements)
15th Antiaircraft Artillery Group
31st and 41st (less 2d Company) Field Antiaircraft Artillery Battalion
3d Field Searchlight Battalion (less 2d Company)
27th Field Machine Cannon Company
2d Field Hospital, 38th Division
Rendova Harbour, Rendova (290)
7th Company (less platoon), III Battalion, 229th Infantry
2d Company, Kure 6th SNLF
Dragons Peninsula, New Georgia
Kure 6th, SNLF (less elements)
2d Battalion (plus 12th Company), 13th Infantry
Kolombangara Sector
13th Infantry (less II Battalion and 12th Company)
58th Field Antiaircraft Artillery Battalion (less company)
22d and 23d Field Machine Cannon Companies
2d Company, 3d Field Searchlight Battery
6th Company, 10th Independent Mountain Artillery
Yokosuka 7th SNLF (less elements)
19th Construction Unit

The Japanese lost 500 men. On August 13 US troops landed on Baanga Island to the west of Munda securing it on the 20th after remnants of the 229th Infantry, III/230 and III/23 Infantry evacuated to Arundel Island. Arundel northwest of Munda was assaulted on August 27 and secured on September 21. Elements of the 230th Infantry defended Arundel. The 13th Infantry was evacuated to Kolombangara on 20 September. The Allies by-passed Kolombangara to aim at Vella Lavella 40 miles to the northwest. The 10,000 Japanese on Kolombangara were evacuated by destroyers to Choiseul and Bougainville on September 28/29 and October 1/2 and 2/3.

The original Allied plan called for 15,000 US troops to defeat 9,000 Japanese with Munda Point secured in 10 days. Over 50,000 US troops were eventually committed and required 35 days of combat. US losses were 1,100 KIA and almost 4,000 WIA.

Villa Airfield on Kolombangara Island just northwest of New Georgia Island. This was typical of the forward Japanese airfields in the Solomons. Strongly defended Kolombangara was by-passed by the Allies and evacuated by the Japanese between September 28 and October 3, 1943.

Vella Lavella was defended by 250 survivors from Munda and marooned sailors. US Army and Marine units landed on August 15 on the south end. This effectively flanked Kolombangara, so II/45 Infantry and a company of the 6th Field Artillery were deployed to small Gizo Island to the southwest of Kolombangara. On the 17th, 390 men of two 13th Infantry companies and an SNLF platoon established a barge staging base on the east side to evacuate the island. Unidentified detachments reinforced the Japanese to 750 troops. A New Zealand brigade landed on the northwest and northeast coasts on September 25. Japanese casualties were light and all were evacuated on October 6/7.

IGHQ directed on August 13 that Bougainville be reinforced while the central Solomons held out until evacuated by early October. Over 12,400 troops were evacuated from Kolombangara on 28/29 September and 1/2 and 2/3 October by destroyers, torpedo boats, and barges. Rekata Bay on Santa Isabel and an outpost on Ganongga Island were evacuated at the same time. The Southeast Detachment was disbanded in December.

Bougainville

Bougainville is the northwestern-most and largest of the Solomons, and is located some 300 miles northwest of Guadalcanal. The Japanese occupied Bougainville and Buka as out-guards for Rabaul. The Shortlands was developed as a forward naval base and used as a staging area for the forays aimed at Guadalcanal. Some 38,000 troops were on the islands: 15,000 at Buin with 1st Base Force including 17th Army Headquarters on nearby Erventa Island; 5,000 of the 17th Infantry Group on Buka Island off the north end along with 87th Guard Force; 5,000 of the 45th Infantry at Kieta; and 1,000 at Mosigetta, mainly involved in rice farming. The 6th Division under MajGen Hyakutke Seikichi was headquartered at Buin with remnants of units evacuated from Guadalcanal. The Shortland Islands off the south end were secured by the IJN. 8th Fleet Headquarters and 1st Base Force were on Faisi Island with 5,000 personnel. Some 6,800 base and Sasebo 6th and Kure 7th SNLF personnel secured nearby Buin and other IJN airfields throughout the area. The 15th Antiaircraft Artillery Group controlled the 38th, 41st, 45th, and 59th Field Antiaircraft Artillery Battalions. Other 17th Army units included the 17th Signals Unit and 2d Shipping Transport Group.

Original Allied plans called for Marine and Army units to seize the Shortlands and Bougainville's south end, but this was cancelled as the area was too heavily defended. Rather than attack the main Japanese position, the 3d Marine Division would land on the remote southwest-central coast at Cape Torokina on the northwest edge of Empress Augusta Bay. A lodgment would be established in which airfields would be built to defend the perimeter and attack Japanese installations in the area including Rabaul. This forced the Japanese to trek long distances from both ends of the island exposing them to air attack and extending their supply lines. The Americans had no intention of securing the entire island.

Besides the main positions, small IJA detachments defended possible landing sites around the island. One such, 2d Company, I Battalion, 23d Infantry, 6th Division, defended Cape Torokina with 270 men. The Marines landed on November 1, 1943 and secured the cape with light casualties; the Japanese suffered almost 200 dead. The US transports withdrew before the IJN cruiser force sent from Rabaul could intercept them, which was itself then intercepted by an American force. 17th Army had expected a landing within three days, but not at Cape Torokina, and believed this was a diversion for the main landing yet to come.

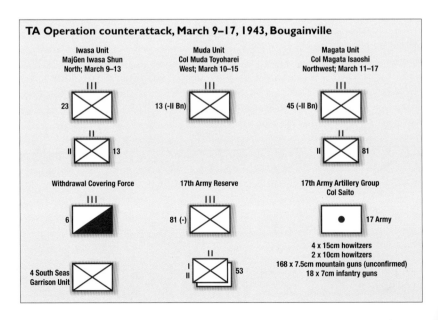

TA Operation counterattack, March 9–17, 1943, Bougainville

Iwasa Unit — MajGen Iwasa Shun — North; March 9–13
23 (III)
II 13

Muda Unit — Col Muda Toyoharei — West; March 10–15
13 (-II Bn) (III)

Magata Unit — Col Magata Isaoshi — Northwest; March 11–17
45 (-II Bn) (III)
II 81

Withdrawal Covering Force
6 (III)
4 South Seas Garrison Unit

17th Army Reserve
81 (-) (III)
I/II 53 (II)

17th Army Artillery Group — Col Saito
17 Army
4 x 15cm howitzers
2 x 10cm howitzers
168 x 7.5cm mountain guns (unconfirmed)
18 x 7cm infantry guns

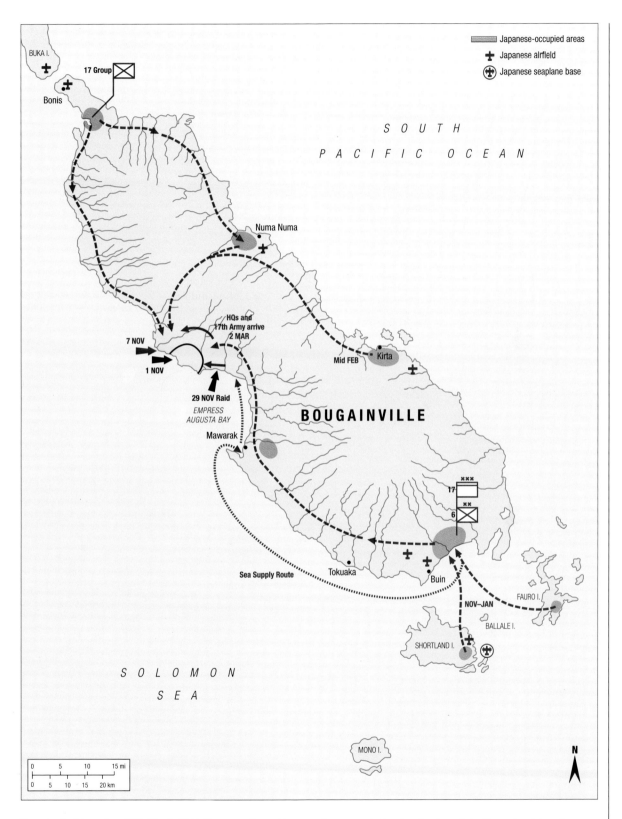

Legend:
- Japanese-occupied areas
- ✚ Japanese airfield
- ⊕ Japanese seaplane base

BUKA I.
✚
Bonis
17 Group ⊠

SOUTH PACIFIC OCEAN

Numa Numa
✚

HQs and
17th Army arrive
2 MAR

7 NOV →
1 NOV →

Mid FEB ● Kirta
✚

29 NOV Raid
EMPRESS
AUGUSTA BAY

Mawarak

BOUGAINVILLE

17 ×××
6 ⊠

✚
Tokuaka
✚
● Buin

Sea Supply Route

FAURO I.

NOV–JAN

BALLALE I.

SHORTLAND I.
✚ ⊕

SOLOMON
SEA

MONO I.

N

0   5   10   15 mi
0   5   10   15   20 km

Bougainville, November 1943–March 1944. Concentrations of Japanese forces are depicted at the time of the November 1 American landing at Cape Torokina. The Japanese deployment routes for the March counteroffensive underline the transportation and logistical difficulties the Japanese faced.

On November 7, 850 troops were ferried from Rabaul and conducted a counterlanding on the Marine left flank with 6th Company, II/53 Infantry; 5th, 6th, 7th (1st Platoon only), and Machine Gun Companies, II/54th Infantry, 17th Division. This force was mostly wiped out by the 9th. Beginning on the 8th additional Marine and Army units arrived to expand the perimeter and construction began on two airfields. The 23d Infantry (less I Battalion) was dispatched from Buin under the 6th Infantry Group commanded by MajGen Iwasa Shun as the Iwasa Detachment. They attacked from the northeast on November 8–9. The Marines were relieved by two Army divisions by mid-December as the lead Japanese forces tried to keep the perimeter from expanding. In November the 17th Division at Rabaul sent 6,000 troops in a field artillery and four infantry battalions to northern Bougainville. The 4th South Seas Garrison Unit with three infantry battalions and field artillery, tankette, and signal companies arrived from China.

In mid-January 1944, 17th Army commenced the TA Operation to eject the Americans from Bougainville. The 6th Division commanded by LtGen Hya with the 13th (less elements), 23d and 45th Infantry; 6th Field Artillery was reinforced by the 17th Division's 53d and 81st Infantry and 10th Mountain Artillery plus a battalion of the 4th Heavy Artillery. The force began training for the offensive; roads were built toward the perimeter from Buin, and supplies built-up. 17th Army had learned on Guadalcanal that small piecemeal attacks on an American perimeter would fail. Almost everything had to be moved overland as most barges were destroyed by US air and naval actions.

Y-Day was March 8 and 11,700 assault troops, backed by 3,700 support troops, attacked from the northwest, north, and northeast. They battered themselves in six attacks against a perimeter defended by 62,000 Americans; the Japanese had underestimated their strength by one half. After losing 5,400 dead and 7,000 wounded the 17th Army began withdrawing on the 25th. The Americans lost fewer than 300 dead. On April 18, 1943 Adm Yamamoto's aircraft was shot down en route from Rabaul to Buin and crashed on nearby Ballele Island.[13]

The Torokina perimeter was reasonably quiet through 1944 and the 31,000 Japanese settled down in their strongholds on both ends of the island. American forces on Bougainville were relieved by Australian troops between October and December 1944.

Eastern New Guinea

Japanese moves to take Eastern New Guinea began in March 1942 when IJA and IJN elements landed at Salamaua, Lae, and Fischhafen on Huon Gulf in Northeast New Guinea. Between April 1 and 20, SNLF troops landed at Fafak, Babo, Sorong, Manokwari, Momi, Nabire, Seroi, Sarmi, and Hollandia along the north coast of New Guinea. The IJN's MO Operation attempted to seize Port Moresby on the south coast of Papua, resulting in the invasion convoy being driven away during the May 4–8 Battle of the Coral Sea. An overland attempt was launched on July 22 when IJA troops landed at Gona on the north coast. The Japanese were driven back on the Kokoda Trail and dug-in at Buna-Gona in late September. (These actions are described in Osprey Battle Orders 9, *Japanese Army in World War II: Conquest of the Pacific 1941–42*.)

Buna-Gona—the battle for the beaches
The battered South Seas Detachment (*Nankai Shitai*) and its attached units under MajGen Horii Tomitaro retreated back north on the Kokoda Trail, and established three defensive perimeters in the Buna-Gona area on the northwest Papua coast on September 24. The surrounding terrain was flat and mostly swampy, forcing the defenders to build most positions above ground or to a

13 Adm Koga Mineichi assumed command of the Combined Fleet.

shallow depth. The forests were dense, but interspaced with open marshes, wet grasslands, and coconut groves. The open areas and airstrips at Buna provided the defenders with clear fields of fire. The South Seas Detachment had actually landed with 300 draft horses, but they were soon eaten.

The easternmost position at Gona was the smallest, less than one mile wide on the beach and half a mile deep. It was defended by IJN personnel and 800 IJA road-building and water-purification troops under Maj Yamamoto Tsume. Besides protecting the east flank it covered the IJA barge anchorage at Basabua less than one mile west. Prior to the Australian attack 100 additional men arrived, consisting of troops from the 41st Infantry and some wounded troops released from hospital.

The Sanananda-Giruwa position lay some 3 1/2 miles east, two miles wide on the beach and half a mile deep. This was the main supply base and held the 67th LoC Hospital with 1,800 sick and wounded plus 500 IJA supply and construction troops. Col Yokoyama Yosuke of the 15th Independent Engineer Regiment was in command; he was also temporary commander of the South Seas Detachment. Three outer positions ("sectors" to the Japanese) were located as far as 3 1/2 miles inland on the main road entering the area; the Japanese collectively called them "South Giruwa." They also blocked tracks cutting off toward Basabua. These positions were under LtCol Tsukamoto Hatsuo commanding I/144 Infantry. In the Southwest Sector Yokoyama positioned 1,800 men of the headquarters; one company, III/41 Infantry; I/144 Infantry (less elements); part of the 15th Engineer; 700 Formosan laborers; and stragglers. In the smaller Central and North Sectors he dug in another company from III/41 Infantry; a company of I/55 Mountain Artillery; 350 troops of the 15th Engineer; and 250 troops of 47th Field Antiaircraft Artillery Battalion (less elements). Col Yokoyama established his headquarters at Giruwa with the 41st Infantry (less elements); a mountain gun company; 3d Company, 55th Cavalry; and 550 men of the IJN 14th and 15th Construction Units. They were reinforced by 800 South Seas Detachment infantry replacements on November 23.

LtGen Adachi Hatazo commanded the 18th Army on Eastern New Guinea from November 1942 until he surrendered his devastated forces at war's end. He was tried for war crimes at Rabaul and sentenced to life imprisonment, but committed suicide in 1947.

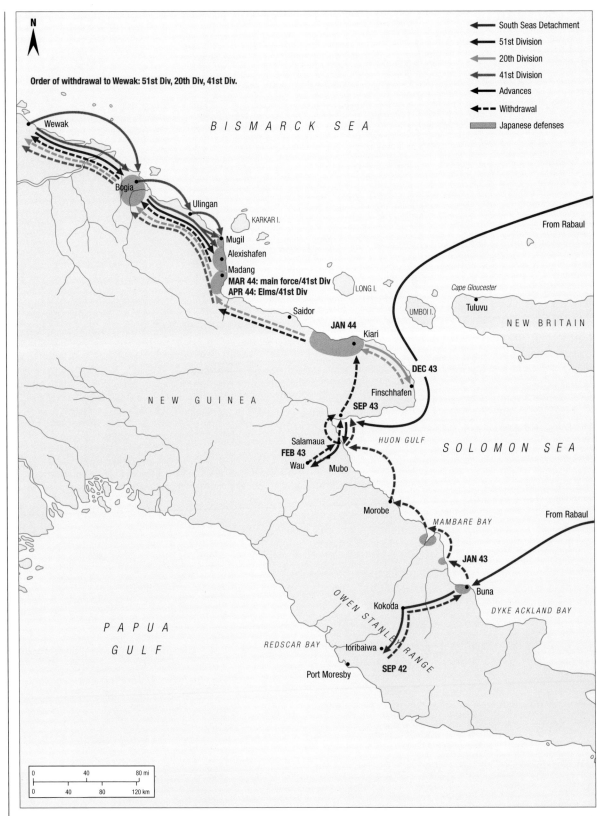

Legend:
- South Seas Detachment
- 51st Division
- 20th Division
- 41st Division
- Advances
- Withdrawal
- Japanese defenses

Order of withdrawal to Wewak: 51st Div, 20th Div, 41st Div.

N

BISMARCK SEA

Wewak

Bogia

Ulingan

KARKAR I.

Mugil

Alexishafen

Madang

MAR 44: main force/41st Div
APR 44: Elms/41st Div

LONG I.

Saidor

JAN 44

Kiari

DEC 43

From Rabaul

Cape Gloucester

Tuluvu

NEW BRITAIN

UMBOI I.

Finschhafen

NEW GUINEA

SEP 43

Salamaua

FEB 43

Wau

Mubo

HUON GULF

SOLOMON SEA

Morobe

MAMBARE BAY

From Rabaul

JAN 43

Buna

DYKE ACKLAND BAY

PAPUA

GULF

Kokoda

OWEN STANLEY RANGE

REDSCAR BAY

Ioribaiwa

SEP 42

Port Moresby

0   40   80 mi
0   40   80   120 km

Japanese movements in Eastern New Guinea, July 1942–April 1944. On this map, different colours have been used to distinguish the units, and refer only to Japanese forces.

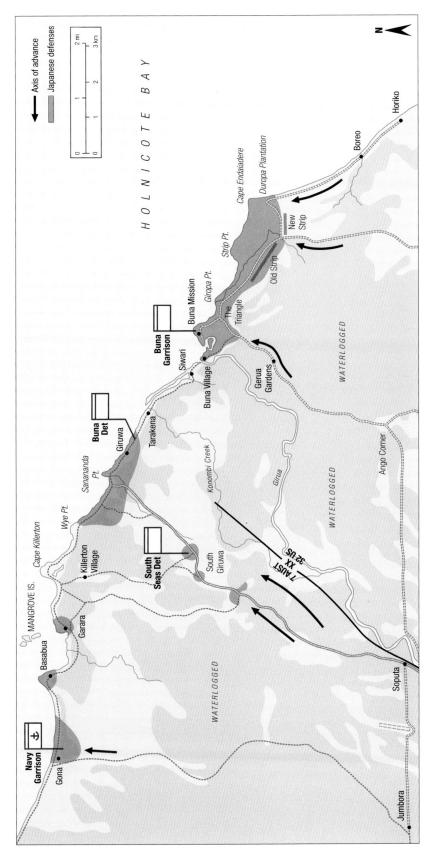

Buna-Gona positions, November 1943–January 1944. In addition to the four main positions (Gona, Sanananda-Giruwa, South Giruwa, and Buna), there were countless small, scattered positions in between. It required seven Australian brigades, four US regiments, and over two months of brutal fighting to reduce Buna-Gona.

Axis of advance

Japanese defenses

2 mi

3 km

HOLNICOTE BAY

Horiko

Boreo

Cape Endaiadere

Duropa Plantation

New Strip

Strip Pt.

Old Strip

Giropa Pt.

Buna Mission

The Triangle

WATERLOGGED

Buna Garrison

Siwari

Buna Village

Gerua Gardens

Ango Corner

Tarakena

Buna Det

Giruwa

Konombi Creek

Girua

WATERLOGGED

Sanananda Pt.

Wye Pt.

Cape Killerton

Killerton Village

South Seas Det

South Giruwa

7 AUST
XX
32 US

MANGROVE IS.

Garara

Basabua

WATERLOGGED

Soputa

Navy Garrison

Gona

Jumbora

75

Japanese prisoners were a rare phenomenon, and were usually exhausted or wounded when captured. Most of those taken prisoner were laborers, and were often Formosans, Okinawans, or Koreans. Here prisoners at Buna, New Guinea are being provided with C-rations.

Less than two miles west was the largest position, Buna, encompassing Buna Village, Buna Mission, the government station, and two airstrips within its 3 1/2-mile-wide, half to three-quarter mile-deep zone. IJN Capt Yasuda Yoshitatsu, commanding Yokosuka 5th SNLF, who arrived September 17, was in charge of all forces east of the Girua River, while Col Yokoyama oversaw those to the west in the absence of MajGen Horii Tomitaro (commander, South Seas Detachment). He positioned a few hundred IJA service and 15th Engineer troops, and a 47th Field Antiaircraft Artillery Battalion company on his east flank defending the Duropa Plantation and the New Strip (actually a dummy strip). The rest of the perimeter was defended by 500 men of the Yokosuka 5th and Sasebo 5th SNLFs, 450 IJN construction troops, plus New Britain forced laborers. The SNLF troops were armed with a few 8cm coast defense guns, 4cm pom-pom guns, and 13.2mm machine guns.

In all there were some 5,500 effectives, including construction troops, in the Buna-Gona area. The remainder of the 41st Infantry (900 men under Col Yazawa Kiyomi and accompanied by MajGen Horii) was still in the mountains to the west retreating north from the Kokoda Trail. Reinforcements were en route from Rabaul. These comprised 700 men of III/229 Infantry and

The New Strip at Buna, littered with the wreckage of IJN Mitsubishi A6M2 Type 0 fighters. This plane was codenamed the "Zeke" by the Allies, but was better known as the "Zero."

300 troops from 144th Infantry replacements with the new regimental commander, Col Yamamoto Hiroshi (aka Shigenori[14]); on arrival, they were sent to Buna, giving it 2,500 combatants. Here Col Hiroshi took command of what was called the Buna Garrison.

The three-pronged Allied attack commenced on November 16 and immediately became bogged down because the troops were already exhausted, the terrain was formidable, the Japanese defenses were well-prepared, rations and ammunition were in short supply, the heat was excessive, and there was nightly rainfall.

Gona and Basabua fell on December 8–9. Over 700 Japanese were buried, but the Australians suffered 750 dead, missing, and wounded. On December 19 MajGen Oda Kensaku arrived to assume command of the South Seas Detachment and established his headquarters in South Giruwa.

The rear guard on the Kokoda Trail, 41st Infantry, reached the mouth of the Kumusi River 12 miles from Gona in late November. MajGen Horii and his chief of staff had drowned crossing the river. Some 500 men of II/41 made it to Gona via barges sent by Col Yokoyama on the 29th, and suffered losses to air attack. On December 2, III/170 Infantry (less elements) of the 21st IMB reached Basabua after I/170 was forced by air attack to return to Rabaul. Only 500 troops of III/170 and the brigade headquarters under MajGen Yamagata Tsuyuo reached shore, and in turn also suffered air attacks. The remnants of I/41 joined them, having marched from the Kumusi River. On the 19th, I/170, a company of III/170, regimental gun company, and 25th Field Machine Cannon Company with 870 men arrived and these units assembled at Napapo northwest of Gona. They would serve as the relief force covering the withdrawal of survivors. MajGen Yamagata moved the relief force by barge to Giruwa December 27–29 and assumed command of all forces in Sanananda-Giruwa and Buna as the Buna Detachment. Under Col Yazawa, the relief force was ordered to launch an attack to support the Buna Garrison on January 1. With American troops penetrating into the Buna perimeter, the commanders at Giruwa and Buna were planning to conduct a suicide attack on the 2nd, the

Japanese coastal defenses, with extensive inland defenses in the form of trenches, rifleman pits, machine-gun positions, pillboxes, and earthworks, were typical of the Buna-Gona area.

14 Col Kusonose Masao was wounded and evacuated from the Kokoto. I/144 commander was in temporary command of the regiment.

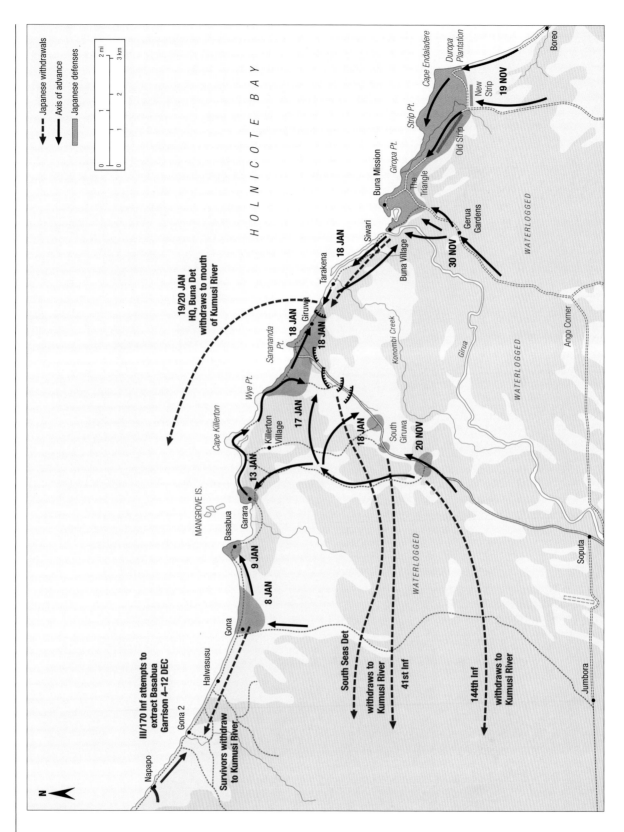

Japanese withdrawals
Axis of advance
Japanese defenses

2 mi
3 km

HOLNICOTE BAY

Boreo

Duropa Plantation
Cape Endaiadere
New Strip
19 NOV
Old Strip
Strip Pt.
Giropa Pt.
Buna Mission
The Triangle
Gerua Gardens
30 NOV
Siwari
Buna Village
WATERLOGGED
Ango Corner
18 JAN
Tarakena
Giruwa
18 JAN
18 JAN
Konombi Creek
Girua
Sanananda Pt.
18 JAN
South Giruwa
18 JAN
20 NOV
Wye Pt.
17 JAN
WATERLOGGED
Cape Killerton
Killerton Village
13 JAN
Soputa
19/20 JAN HQ, Buna Det withdraws to mouth of Kumusi River
South Seas Det withdraws to Kumusi River
41st Inf
144th Inf withdraws to Kumusi River
MANGROVE IS.
Basabua
Garara
9 JAN
8 JAN
WATERLOGGED
Gona
Halwasusu
Jumbora
III/170 Inf attempts to extract Basabua Garrison 4–12 DEC
Gona 2
Napapo
Survivors withdraw to Kumusi River

N

The withdrawal from Buna-Gona, January 1943. Some elements of those units destroyed here managed to escape 20 miles west to the Kumusi River, or were evacuated by barge. The fact that some 3,400 managed to escape was unknown to the Allies.

A trench system and machine-gun pillbox at Buna. Camouflage has been removed by the photographer from this position to show it more clearly. This image demonstrates that such positions were built in densely vegetated terrain. Although this restricted observation and fields of fire, it made the positions extremely difficult to detect.

date the garrison crumbled, though many men held out. The relief force fought to within one mile of Buna, where on the 8th, a few hundred survivors linked up and they withdrew to Giruwa. Buna was in Allied hands, at a cost of 1,500 Japanese dead and 2,750 Allied dead, missing, and wounded.

Allied attacks on Sanananda-Giruwa continued relentlessly, but slowly. IGHQ concluded that holding both Guadalcanal and Sanananda-Giruwa was impossible and it was decided to evacuate both. On January 13, 18th Army ordered the evacuation of Sanananda-Giruwa with the Australians pushing in from the south and the Americans from the east. I/170 was annihilated holding off the American attack while the Australians destroyed many of the defenders of South Giruwa. The end came on January 21. Almost 2,000 Japanese were buried in the area, and the Allies lost 3,500 dead, missing, and wounded.

Headquarters of the Buna Detachment and assorted troops were evacuated by barge on December 19/20 while other defenders of Sanananda-Giruwa and South Giruwa managed to escape west overland, with survivors assembling on

Blasted terrain at Buna Mission. The native thatch hut concealed a Japanese pillbox.

the Kumusi River. Between December 13 and 20, 1,190 sick and wounded were evacuated by barge. Some 3,400 troops were assembled by February 7, far more than the Allies had thought escaped, and were shuttled by barge to Salamaua and Lae by mid-March. The survivors were starved, exhausted, and ill, but most were absorbed into the recently arrived 51st Division.

It was an exceedingly brutal campaign for both sides, and burying the thousands of men who died during the action proved almost impossible. The numbers of Japanese buried by the Allies provides misleading casualty figures. The best estimate is that 12,000 of the 16–17,000 Japanese committed to Buna-Gona died, and 350 prisoners were taken. In all 4,500 troops were evacuated.

Northeast New Guinea

Just over 200 miles northwest of Buna lies the Huon Peninsula enclosing the Huon Gulf near the southeast end of Northeast New Guinea. On March 8, II/144 Infantry and a mountain artillery company from the South Seas Detachment landed at Salamaua, while the Maizuru 2d SNLF seized Lae. II/144 was relieved by the 1,300-man 82d Guard Force under Cmdr Miyata Kashin to defend the area. The Japanese needed this terrain for airfields to support the move on Port Moresby.

Additional reinforcements were arriving further to the north in December 1942. This effort was to protect the Damipier and Vitiaz Straits separating New Britain and the Huon Peninsula, to back the Lae-Salamaua forces, and to support a resumption of the offensive to control Papua. Madang was occupied by two infantry battalions and Wewak by one, all from the 5th Division on Amboina Island southwest of New Guinea. The 11th, 21st, and 42d Infantry each donated a battalion. The 5th Division was under 16th Army control, but 8th Area Army transferred the battalions to 18th Army control. On the 12th, a Sasebo 5th SNLF company occupied Fischhafen on the Huon Peninsula.

Small Australian units had harassed the Japanese at Lae-Salamaua from the moment they landed, but the 3,000-man Okabe Detachment from the 51st Division, arriving January 7, 1943, attacked Wau 35 miles southwest of Salamaua on the 28th. By the end of February the Australians, now reinforced, had pushed the Japanese two-thirds of the way back.

Okabe Detachment, MajGen Okabe Tooru
HQ, 51st Infantry Group
102d Infantry (less III Battalion[1])
II Battalion (less one company), 14th Field Artillery
3d Company, 51st Engineer
company, 51st Transport
field machine cannon company
medical unit
[1] Most of III Battalion was lost, returned to Rabaul, or used as stevedores at Lae after their transport sank.

The 18th Army attempted to reinforce them at the end of February by sending 6,900 troops of the 51st Division to Salamaua; but half the force was lost during the 3–4 March Battle of the Bismarck Sea, and the 2,427 survivors returned to Rabaul, among them the commander of 18th Army. Only 800 troops reached Lae with LtGen Nakano Hidemitau of the 51st Division. He took command of forces in the Lae-Salamau area, and the survivors of Buna-Gona assembled here in late March. Despite this reinforcement, the Australians and Japanese had reached a stalemate.

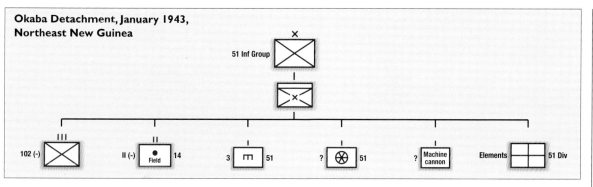

Okaba Detachment, January 1943, Northeast New Guinea

51 Inf Group

102 (-)	II (-) 14 Field	3 51	? 51	? Machine cannon	Elements 51 Div

51st Division (less elements), LtGen Nakano Hidemitau
HQ, 51st Division
115th Infantry (less elements), Col Endo Torahei
14th Artillery (less elements)
51st Engineer, Lt Col Hondo
51st Division Signals Unit
3d Field Hospital
8th Shipping Engineer Regiment
Elements of 15th Independent Engineer
50th Field Antiaircraft Artillery Battalion (less one company)
3d Debarkation Unit
3d Company, 5th Shipping Engineer Regiment
Elements of 5th Air Signals Regiment
22d and 209th Airfield Battalions

The interior of a Japanese bunker at Buna. This bunker is a bomb shelter and not a fighting position. It is heavily constructed of coconut palms and sand-filled fuel drums.

18th Army, LtGen Adachi Hatazo
HQ, 18th Army, LtGen Yoshihara Kane (Chief of Staff)
20th Division
41st Division
51st Division
18th Army Signals Troops
6th Independent Antitank Battalion
2d, 21st Mortar Battalions [9cm]
50th, 56th, 58th (less elements), 61st–63d Field Antiaircraft Artillery Battalions
38th–41st Independent Antiaircraft Artillery Companies
25th, 29th Field Machine Cannon Companies
1st–4th, 6th, 7th Independent Field Searchlight Companies
HQ, 4th Engineer Unit, MajGen Yamada Shigeru
8th, 30th, 33d, 36th, 37th Independent Engineer
35th–38th, 40th, 44th, 48th Road Construction Units
3d, 4th Field Transport Commands
3d Independent Transport Regiment
39th, 42d Transport Battalions
225th, 263d, 290th, 291st, 302d, 304th Independent Transport Companies
1st–12th, 16th–18th Special Independent Transport Companies[1]
1st Shipping Transport Group
5th, 9th Shipping Engineer Regiments

[1] Manned largely by Koreans and Formosans.

Within III/115 Infantry, the remnants of the 9th, 11th, and 12th companies were consolidated into the 9th Mixed Company alongside the mostly intact 10th Company. This battalion was delivered on March 20. Subsequent attempts to send the 66th Infantry in April failed. The remainder of the 51st Division arrived in June, giving a total of 7,200 troops.

On December 23, 1942 IGHQ had ordered two divisions, the 20th in Korea and the 41st in North China, to the Solomons. After it was decided to evacuate Guadalcanal on January 4 they were assigned to 18th Army and sent to New Guinea. A simple analysis of the support units indicates the Japanese were planning to undertake a major road-building effort, make available ample supply transport, and provide increased air defense—inadequate factors in the Solomons.

With the 20th, 41st, and 51st divisions, 18th Army numbered 100,000 troops. However, the divisions were deployed much understrength, leaving rear echelons and even some units, including most artillery, in rear areas. The 41st Division, for example, deployed with 13,700 troops out of its 20,000. The 51st Division would reinforce Lae-Salamaua, 20th Division would land at Madang and advance toward Lae-Salamaua constructing a 135-mile-long supply road, and 41st Division would land at Wewak and later advance to Madang. The deployments taxed Japanese shipping, but the 20th Division was delivered intact on January 19 and the 41st Division arrived February 20–28, both spared of air attacks. The 8th Area Army placed increased emphasis and the 6th Air Division would advance its bases to New Guinea with its headquarters at Wewak. The much-needed Madang-Lae supply road was not begun until April though, and proved to be an almost impossible task. Only 40 miles had been completed by June.

20th Division, LtGen Katagiri Shigeru
HQ, 20th Division
HQ, 20th Infantry Group, MajGen Nakai Masutaro
78th Infantry
79th Infantry
80th Infantry
26th Field Artillery (less elements)
20th Reconnaissance
20th Engineer
20th Transport
20th Division Signals Unit
20th Ordnance Duty Unit
20th Medical Unit
41st Division, LtGen Mano Goro
HQ, 41st Division
HQ, 41st Infantry Group, MajGen Shoge Ryoichi
237th Infantry
238th Infantry
239th Infantry
41st Mountain Artillery (less elements)
41st Reconnaissance
41st Engineer
41st Transport
41st Division Signals Unit
41st Ordnance Duty Unit
41st Medical Unit

An IJN air offensive, I Operation, began on April 7 with attacks throughout the Solomons and New Guinea. The 18th Army commander finally managed to make it to Madang on April 19. The Allies were preparing six divisions for further offensive operations and building more airfields. In early June the 51st Division's 66th Infantry (Surudoi Detachment) made it to Lae, though elements of the battered division remained at Rabaul. The Japanese had 20,000 troops at Wewak (41st Division, 6th Air Division, 2d Special Base Force), 20,000 at Madang (18th Army, 20th Division), and 15,000 at Lae-Salamaua-Fischhafen (51st Division, 7th Base Force). In July the 7th Air Division in the NEI was assigned to 8th Area Army and then the headquarters of 4th Air Army under LtGen Oyokawa Furushio.

On June 20 the 66th Infantry attacked Australian positions at Gaudagasal, but was driven back to Mubo. Australian and US forces commenced an offensive on June 30 coinciding with the Rendova landing. The American landing at Nassau Bay 10 miles south of Salamaua surprised the 51st Division, which was dug in to face a land attack from Gaudagasal. While the 51st Division order of battle appears impressive, most units were understrength or incomplete, and it totaled only 7,200[15]. The flexibility of Japanese command arrangements is demonstrated by the situation in the Lae-Salamaua area. The

---

15 The division's 51st Reconnaissance Regiment was on New Britain and the 51st Transport Regiment was with the Marcus Island occupation force in the Bismarcks.

51st Division, LtGen Nakano Hidemitau
HQ, 51st Division
HQ, 51st Infantry Group, MajGen Mutotani Chuichi
66th Infantry
102d Infantry
115th Infantry
14th Field Artillery (less elements)
51st Engineer
II Battalion, 21st Infantry, 5th Division
I Battalion, 80th Infantry, 20th Division
15th, 30th Independent Engineer
5th Independent Heavy Artillery Battalion
Company, 50th Field Antiaircraft Artillery Battalion
3d Field Hospital
7th Base Force
Sasebo 5th SNLF (less elements)
82d Guard Force

51st Division commander was in overall command, but in order to allow him to concentrate on the defense of Salamaua, the 41st Infantry Group Headquarters from the 41st Division was sent to command the garrison and service units at Lae. The Australian inland flanking movement drove the 51st Division back to Salamaua by the end of September. The 51st Infantry Group with its own I/66 and 20th Division's I/80 had attempted to meet this threat. 18th Army determined that Salamaua must be held or Lae was worthless.

Australian and US reinforcements arrived and the offensive continued, forcing the 51st Division to contract its front and fall back. Japanese goals were still ambitious, with plans to attack Allied airfields being built in the mountains with the 20th and 41st Divisions. By September though, after fresh Australian troops relieved the original force, the Japanese defense was crumbling. On September 4 an Australian division landed 18 miles south of Lae and at the same time a US parachute regiment dropped onto Nadzab airfield 12 miles west of Lae to close off an escape route. An Australian division was airlifted in and began advancing east toward Lae. On September 2, 8th Area Army ordered 18th Army to delay at Lae-Salamaua and for new defenses to be established in the Dampier Strait area (Booke Island and west end of New Britain). Between September 11 and 14, the Japanese abandoned Salamaua and retreated along the coast as other troops evacuated by barge to Lae. They were reinforced by a battalion of the 102d Infantry and Sasebo 5th SNLF, making a total of 9,085 troops. The Allies attempted to cut off the 51st Division, but over 9,000 IJA and IJN troops escaped north over the Huon Peninsula's mountains on September 12–15. The 20th Infantry Group with 78th Infantry and I/26 Field Artillery (Nakai Detachment) had been moved up by the 20th Division to the west to cover the 51st's withdrawal, but it was pulled back to defend the approaches to Madang since the 51st did not take that route. The defense and retreat from Lae-Salamaua cost the Japanese 2,600 men.

On September 30 the IGHQ designated a new National Defense Zone anchored in the Marianas, running through the Carolines, then through Dutch New Guinea, and on the south edge of the NEI (Sumatra, Java, Timor) to the south facing Australia. This was forced by the loss of the Solomons and the Aleutians. Japanese forces in the Bismarcks and eastern New Guinea were no

Yamada Detachment, MajGen Yamada Eizo
HQ, 1st Shipping Transport Group
80th Infantry (less I Battalion and 5th Company)
II Battalion, 238th Infantry
Battalion of 26th Field Artillery
Elements of 1st Shipping Transport Group
Elements of 7th Base Force (500)

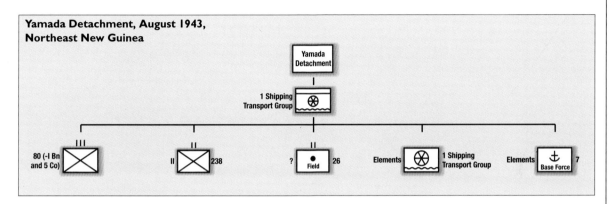

Yamada Detachment, August 1943, Northeast New Guinea

longer a part of the Empire's perimeter defense, but would fight delaying actions while new defenses were established to the north and west. In early November the 7th Air Division was sent back to Amboina to help establish the National Defense Zone. To defend Finschhafen on the east end of the Huon Peninsula, 18th Army formed the Yamada Detachment on August 7 under the 1st Shipping Transport Group commander.

The 20th Division was relieved of Madang-Lae road construction on September 10 and ordered to Finschhafen. Lacking vehicles and horses, and travelling on a crude track, it was still 100 miles away from its destination a month later.

20th Division, September–December 1943
79th Infantry
26th Field Artillery (less two battalions)
20th Engineer
33d Independent Engineer
Divisional service elements

On September 22 Australian troops landed 5½ miles north of Finschhafen while a smaller force followed the peninsula's south coast around from Lae to approach from the south. The Japanese put up stiff resistance on the inland mountains and were not routed until December 8. The Yamada Detachment and 20th Division linked up with the Lae-Salamaua survivors, withdrew north, and then along the north coast. The next step up the New Guinea coast for the Allies was Saidor, almost 90 miles from Finschhafen. A US force landed there on January 2, 1944 to block the retreating Japanese. The Americans expected the Japanese to attack Saidor, but Australian intelligence felt they would by-pass rather than attack Saidor, which they did. Three Allied divisions were now in pursuit of the retreating 18th Army, which made it to Madang in early April

The Japanese-built footbridge at Buna, giving an idea of the swampy terrain encountered there.

with the remnants of the 51st and 20th Divisions, attachments, and IJN personnel—10,000 men in total. They continued up the coast though, and Australians entered Madang on April 24. 18th Army continued to retreat, abandoning Wewak, over 200 miles from Madang, and continued on to Dutch New Guinea. The commander of the 51st Division was in overall command of both divisions as the Nakano Group; the 18th Army commander was taken by submarine to Madang. On May 10 the 20th Division commander was killed and MajGen Nakai Masutaro of the 20th Infantry Group took over.

The last major US action on Eastern New Guinea was at Aitape, almost 100 miles from Wewak, when US troops landed there on April 22. This was conducted at the same time as the Hollandia landings 125 miles to the west in Dutch New Guinea. Some 3,500 construction, supply, and air service personnel plus 20th Division replacements under the 44th LoC Unit commanded by Col Ujihara occupied this airbase and logistics base area. They withdrew when the Americans landed.

With Apitape and Hollandia occupied, 18th Army was cut off from Japanese bases in western New Guinea. Its three divisions and support troops numbered 55,000 with 3,000 hospitalized. Artillery companies generally had one gun apiece. The 18th Army decided to move west without orders. Some 20,000 men, including 51st Division, remained to defend Wewak while the rest headed west toward Apitape. The two sides probed each other as the Americans built up forces in expectation of the advancing and desperate 18th Army, which was low on rations. On the night of July 10/11, 78th and 80th Infantry, 20th Division and 237th Infantry, 41st Division penetrated the American line on the Driniumor River and pushed them back to a second line. The American line was restored by the beginning of August.

The battered 20th and 41st divisions withdrew to Wewak after losing 8,000 men to combat and illness; most regiments barely numbered above 300 men. Australian forces relieved the Americans in November to contain 18th Army at

Effective strength of 20th and 41st Divisions, July 1944	
20th Division	41st Division
78th Infantry (1,300)	237th Infantry (3,240)
79th Infantry (700, two battalions)	238th Infantry (two battalions[1])
80th Infantry (1,010)	239th Infantry (1,842)
26th Field Artillery (990)	41st Mountain Artillery (1,427)
	66th Infantry (1,000)[2]

[1] Strength unknown, employed as porters.
[2] Attached from 51st Division as porters; only III/66 was combat effective.

Wewak. The army had been reduced to 35,000 men and was scattered in small groups over a wide area west of Wewak, Wewak itself, and well inland. This was necessary in order to live off the land and tend gardens.

The Australians placed pressure on the Japanese through early 1945 and stepped up attacks. The Japanese were forced into the mountains, and Wewak was secured by the end of May. The 18th Army was down to 13,500 battered and starving troops hemmed in on both sides by Australians. The three divisions each had the strength of less than a regiment. To the south lay hundreds of miles of disease-ridden jungles and mountains. The Japanese withered in the jungles until surrendering at war's end. With the addition of reinforcing units and replacements, an estimated 100,000 Japanese died in eastern New Guinea.

Lessons learned

The Japanese did not make major organizational changes at this stage of the war. They did tailor units for specific missions and terrain, but a major factor affecting this process was extremely limited space available on Japanese shipping. Another issue was the desire to limit the number of ships exposed to Allied air and sea attack, both of which were taking significant tolls. Conserving shipping was essential for ensuring the continued deployment of troops and for supplying them; it was also soon realized that shipping would be necessary for evacuation purposes. Consequently, units were deployed with a reduced number of crew-served weapons, equipment, and ammunition, and weapons crews were reduced. This resulted in limiting each weapon's mobility; there was little or no motor transport on the islands, due to limited shipping space or the lack of roads, and manpower was often insufficient to move weapons and ammunition. It was quickly found on New Guinea that horses, acclimatized to Japan and China, could not survive in the tropics. The fodder that the horses required also took up more shipping space, and required transportation once ashore, as well as additional horse handlers. Troops also needed rations, so units were reduced to the bare minimum, with administrative and service personnel left behind in rear echelons. Moving supplies forward to the front was a major effort, and the inability to do so cost the Japanese greatly. The 17th Army staff assessed that for every 10 units of supplies planned, six were shipped, two made it ashore, and two were delivered to troops. A man tasked with backpacking 10 days rations for a frontline soldier from the debarkation point to the front and back again would require a similar quantity of supplies for himself.

The IJA Shipping Transport Troops played a critical role in the South Pacific. Their transports, coastal freighters, landing barges, and other craft, as well as their debarkation skills and stevedores, were essential. They deployed units, supplied island bases, moved troops along the coast (rather then wearing them out with cross-country marches), and provided a means of evacuation. Any

Japanese fighting positions on the Gifu, a strongly defended hill position west of Henderson Field. The terrain was broken and jumbled, and the positions well concealed among the dense vegetation. US Army attacks on this position began on December 24, 1942, but it did not fall until January 24, 1943. To the left is an LMG position with a rifleman's pit forward of it, protecting it from approach on its blind side.

losses to these troops were keenly felt, and the Japanese soon learned to establish en-route, barge staging bases, where barges stopped during the day and crews and troops rested and made repairs.

The Japanese became proficient in complex and dangerous evacuation operations. They were extremely successful in taking large numbers of troops off Guadalcanal, New Georgia, Kolobangara, Buna, and Salamaua, among others. They were sometimes less successful in delivering troops to islands, being frequently interdicted. One reason is that the Allies were on the lookout for deployments, while they usually were taken by surprise by evacuations. Another reason is that it took much longer to debark troops, equipment, and supplies than to embark them, principally because most of their weapons and supplies were left behind.

The Japanese were inadequately prepared to deal with massive Allied firepower, from both ground and air. They deployed with insufficient air defenses and artillery, making them vulnerable to air attack and counterfire. They were also poorly armed for antitank defense. However, the Allies employed few tanks; when they did employ them, they proved valuable though not necessarily decisive. This was largely due to the extremely rugged terrain, which hampered tank operations. The Japanese misinterpreted the limited use of tanks, though, and were surprised when they were employed in larger numbers and with heavier tanks in 1944.

On a more positive note, the widespread Japanese use of specially tailored "detachments," often put together from any available units from different commands, demonstrated flexibility in command and control. A key aspect of this was the ability of officers to work under commanders outside their normal chain-of-command. Perhaps the most important lessons learned were jungle warfare skills, small-unit tactics in close terrain, fieldcraft, and field sanitation. These skills were passed on to other commands, and put to good use in the years ahead.

IJN personnel assist exhausted IJA troops during the February 1–8, 1943 evacuation of Guadalcanal. Over 10,600 troops were successfully evacuated. Some 80 Daihatsu barges, 100 smaller Shohatsu barges, and 300 collapsible boats were used to transfer troops from shore to 21 destroyers involved in the operation. (Kenichi Nakamura)

Chronology

1942

23 January	Japanese forces land on New Britain and New Ireland.
19 February	Darwin (Australia) is bombed by the Japanese.
4–8 March	Battle of the Coral Sea. The IJN Port Moresby invasion force withdraws.
8 March	Japanese forces seize Lae-Salamaua, New Guinea.
11 March	Japanese forces seize Finschhafen, New Guinea.
24 April	The Doolittle Raid is conducted on Tokyo.
4 May	The IJN seizes Tulagi and Gavutu, in the Solomons.
Spring	Japan activates seven new security divisions.
4–5 June	The Battle of Midway.
9 June	The last US-Filipino forces surrender in Philippines.
13–21 June	Attu and Kiska, in the Aleutian Islands, are seized by Japan.
25 June	Australians land at Milne Bay, Papua.
4 July	A Japanese airfield is discovered on Guadalcanal.
11 July	Japan cancels the invasions of Fiji, New Caledonia, and Samoa.
22 July	The Japanese land at Gona and attempt to seize Port Moresby overland. The Battle for the Kokoda Trail continues until September.
7 August	US Marines assault Guadalcanal-Tulagi.
11 August	Battle of Savo Island ends with an IJN victory.
13 August	Japanese forces land at Buna.
18 August	Japanese commence "KA" Operation to drive US troops from Guadalcanal.
24 August	Battle of the Eastern Solomons.
25 August	The Japanese Milne Bay assault fails.
24 September	The Japanese defense of Buna-Gona begins.
9 October	17th Army HQ arrives on Guadalcanal.
11 October	Battle of Cape Esperance.
13 October	First US Army units arrive on Guadalcanal.
13–15 October	Naval battle of Guadalcanal and IJA offensive.
24 October	Japanese offensive, Battle for Henderson Field, Guadalcanal.
26 October	Battle of Santa Cruz ends in an IJN victory.
13 November	Japanese forces occupy Munda Point, New Georgia.
16 November	Australian/US forces begin their attacks on Buna-Gona.
18 November	Battle of Tassafaronga.
9 December	Gona falls.

1943

2 January	Buna falls.
19 January	20th Division arrives at Madang.
21 January	Sanananda-Giruwa falls. The US occupies the Russell Islands.
1–8 February	The Japanese successfully evacuate Guadalcanal.
20–28 February	41st Division arrives at Wewak.
2–4 March	Battle of the Bismarck Sea. The first elements of 51st Division arrive at Salamaua.
19 April	18th Army HQ arrives at Madang.
21 June	US assault on New Georgia Group commences.
30 June	US secures Rendova Island, New Georgia Group.
2 July	US lands on New Georgia Island to assault Munda Point.
3 August	US secures Munda Point.

13 August	US assaults Baanga Island, New Georgia Group.
15 August	US secures Vella Lavella, New Georgia Group.
27 August	US assaults Arundel Island, New Georgia Group.
3 September	Australians assault Huon Peninsula, New Guinea.
10 September	Australians assault Finschhafen, New Guinea.
14 September	Salamaua abandoned by the Japanese.
25 September	New Zealand forces land on Arundel.
28 September– **3 October**	Japanese successfully evacuate Kolobangara, New Georgia Group.
30 September	Japan establishes a new National Defense Zone, resulting in a major reorganization of forces.
6 October	Battle of Vella Lavella. US secures Kolobangara.
1 November	US assaults Cape Torokina, Bougainville.
7 November	US Army units arrive on Bougainville.
10 December	Australians relieve US units on Bougainville.

1944

2 January	US assaults Saidor, New Guinea.
8 March	Japanese offensive on Bougainville.
22 April	US assaults Aitape and Hollandia, New Guinea.
24 April	Mandang is seized by the Australians.

Bibliography

Cook, Taya and Theodore F. *Japan at War: An Oral History*. New York: The New Press, 1992.

Daugherty, Leo J., III *Fighting Techniques of a Japanese Infantryman, 1941–1945: Training, Techniques, and Weapons*. St. Paul, MN: MBI Publishing, 2002.

Dexter, David *Australia in the War of 1939-1945, The New Guinea Offensives*. Canberra: Australian War Memorial, 1961.

Forty, George *Japanese Army Handbook, 1939–1945*. Stroud, UK: Sutton Publishing, 1999.

Frank, Richard B *Guadalcanal: The Definitive Account of the Landmark Battle*. New York: Random House, 1990.

Fuller, Richard *Shokan—Hirohito's Samurai: Leaders of the Japanese Armed Forces 1926–1945*. London: Arms and Armour Press, 1992.

Gailey, Harry A. *MacArthur's Victory: The War In New Guinea 1943–1944*. New York: Random House, 2004.

Harris, Meirion and Susie *Soldiers of the Sun: the Rise and Fall of the Imperial Japanese Army*. New York: Random House, 1991.

Hayashi, Saburo and Coox, Alvin D *Kogun: The Japanese Army in the Pacific War*. Quantico, VA: Marine Corps Association, 1959. (Published in Japan in 1951 as *Taiheiyo Senso Rikusen Gaishi*.)

Hough, LtCol Frank O.; Ludwig, Maj Verle E.; and Shaw, Henry I. Jr. *History of US Marine Corps Operations in World War II: Pearl Harbor to Guadalcanal*. Vol. I. Washington, DC: US Government Printing Office, 1958.

Icnaga, Saburo *The Pacific War, 1931–1945: A Critical Perspective of Japan's Role in World War II*. New York: Random House, 1978.

Kruger, Walter *From Down Under to Nippon: The Story of the Sixth Army in World War II*. Washington, DC: Zenger Publishing, 1953.

Long, Gavin M. *The Six Years War: A Concise History of Australia in the 1939–1945 War*. Canberra: The Australian War Memorial and the Australian Government Publishing Service, 1973.

McCarthy, Dudley *Australia in the War of 1939–1945, South-West Pacific Area— First Year: Kokoda to Wau*. Canberra: Australian War Memorial, 1959.

Miller, John Jr. *United States Army in World War II: Guadalcanal: The First Offensive*. Washington, DC: US Government Printing Office, 1949.

Miller, John Jr. *Cartwheel: The Reduction of Rabaul*. Washington, DC: US Government Printing Office, 1984.

Milner, Samuel *United States Army in World War II: Victory in Papua*. Washington, DC: US Government Printing Office, 1957.

Morison, Samuel E. *History of US Navy Operations in World War II: Coral Sea, Midway and Submarine Actions May 1942–August 1942*. Vol. IV. Boston: Little, Brown and Co., 1949.

Morison, Samuel E. *History of US Navy Operations in World War II: the Struggle for Guadalcanal August 1942–February 1943*. Vol. V. Boston: Little, Brown and Co., 1949.

Morison, Samuel E. *History of US Navy Operations in World War II: Breaking the Bismarcks Barrier 22 July 1942–1 May 1944*. Vol. VI. Boston: Little, Brown and Co., 1950.

Morison, Samuel E. *History of US Navy Operations in World War II: Aleutians, Gilberts and Marshalls June 1942–April 1944*. Vol. VII. Boston: Little, Brown and Co., 1951.

Morison, Samuel E. *History of US Navy Operations in World War II: New Guinea and the Marianas, March 1944 August 1944*. Vol. VIII. Boston: Little, Brown and Co., 1953.

Rottman, Gordon L. *US Marine Corps Order of Battle: Ground and Air Units in the Pacific War, 1939–1945*. Westport, CT: Greenwood Publishing, 2002.

Rottman, Gordon L. *World War II Pacific Island Guide: A Geo-Military Study*. Westport, CT: Greenwood Publishing, 2002.

Shaw, Henry I. Jr. and Kane, Maj Douglas T. *History of US Marine Corps Operations in World War II: Isolation of Rabual*. Vol. II. Washington, DC: US Government Printing Office, 1963.

Smith, Robert R. *United States Army in World War II: the Approach to the Philippines*. Washington, DC: US Government Printing Office, 1984.

Taaffe, Stephen R. *MacArthur's Jungle War: The 1944 New Guinea Campaign*. Kansas City: University Press of Kansas, 1998.

Toland, John *The Rising Sun: the Decline and Fall of the Japanese Empire, 1939–1945*. New York: Random House, 1970.

War Department, *Handbook on Japanese Military Forces, TM-E 30-480, 15 September 1944*, with Changes 3 and 5, 1 June 1945.

Abbreviations and linear measurements

Abbreviations

AAA	antiaircraft artillery
AT	antitank
Bn	Battalion
Co	Company
CSNLF	Combined Special Naval Landing Force (IJN)
Det	Detachment
Div	Division
Elm	Element
FA	Field Artillery
HMG	heavy machine gun
HQ	Headquarters
IGHQ	Imperial General Headquarters
IIB	Independent Infantry Battalion
IMB	Independent Mixed Brigade
IMR	Independent Mixed Regiment
IJA	Imperial Japanese Army
IJN	Imperial Japanese Navy
LMG	light machine gun
LoC	line-of-communications (when referring to a unit)
NCO	non-commissioned officer
NEI	Netherlands East Indies
SNLF	Special Naval Landing Force (IJN)
US	United States
(-)	less elements detached from unit
(+)	reinforced (additional elements attached)

Officer rank abbreviations and equivalents

Imperial Japanese Army		US Army and Marine Corps	Commonwealth Armies
SubLt	Sub-Lieutenant	2d Lieutenant	2nd-Lieutenant
Lt	Lieutenant	1st Lieutenant	Lieutenant (Lt)
Capt	Captain	Captain	Captain
Maj	Major	Major	Major
LtCol	Lieutenant Colonel	Lieutenant Colonel	Lieutenant-Colonel
Col	Colonel	Colonel	Colonel
MajGen	Major General	Brigadier General (1-star)	Brigadier (Brig)
LtGen	Lieutenant General	Major General (2-star)	Major-General
–	–	Lieutenant General (3-star)	Lieutenant-General
Gen	General	General (4-star)	General
FldMars	Field Marshal	–	Field Marshal

Distances, ranges, and dimensions are mostly given in the contemporary US system of inches, feet, yards, and statute miles. Weapon calibers are given in the standard Japanese metric system, together with other technical specifications relating to types of equipment and *matériel*. A simple conversion table is provided below.

feet to meters:	multiply feet by 0.3048
yards to meters	multiply yards by 0.9114
miles to kilometers	multiply miles by 1.6093
centimeters to inches	multiply centimeters by 0.3937

Index

References to illustrations are shown in **bold**.

Adachi Hatazo, LtGen **73**
Admiralty Islands 49
Air Armies, 1st–3rd 26
Air Army, 4th 26, 44
Air Division, 7th 85
Air Service deployment (July 1942) 26
Air Service flying units 25
air services 24–26
aircraft, Mitsubishi A6M2 Type 0 "Zeke/Zero" **76**
airfields 28
Aleutian Islands 10
Allied strength 48
Amphibious Brigades, 1st–4th 7
antiaircraft artillery battalion, field 23–24
    Type C 23
Antiaircraft Artillery Group, 15th 70
antiaircraft units 22–24
antitank units 19–20
Aoba Detachment 52–53, 54
Army, 2d 8, 43–44
Army, 8th Area 43, 44, 82, 84
Army, 17th 10, 22, 42, 43, 52, 56, 58, 60, 64, 70, 72, 88
    HQ 61, 64, 70
Army, 18th 22, **33**, 43, 44, 79, 80, 82, 84, 85–87
Army, 19th 44
Army, Southern 4, 42, 43
"Army-Navy Central Agreement" 42
artillery battalion, field antiaircraft 23–24
    Type C 23
artillery battalion, independent mountain 21
    20th 22
Artillery Regiment, 10th Independent Mountain 22
Artillery Regiment, 21st Medium 22
artillery regiments, Type C independent medium 20, 22
artillery tactics 34
artillery units 20–22
Australia 10
Australians 30, 80, 86, 87

Bismarck Sea, Battle of the 80
boat, Type F collapsible **45**
Bougainville 28, 30, 69, 70, **71**, 72
Brigade, 65th 11, 18
brigade equivalents 16, 18
Brigades, 1st and 2d Guards 19
Buna Detachment 77, 79–80
Buna-Gona, Eastern New Guinea 36, 72–73, **75**, 76–77, **78**, 79–80
    Buna Mission **79**
    bunker, Japanese **81**
    footbridge, Japanese-built **86**

Gona defenses **28**, **32**
    New Strip airfield **76**
    Sanananda-Giruwa position **29**, 73, 79
    trench system and machine-gun pillbox **79**

camouflage 30–31
China 18
code names and numbers 13
combat experience of units 30
Combined Special Naval Landing Force, 8th 65
command and control, Southeast Area 42–44, **44**
communications 44–46
Coral Sea, Battle of the 72
cultural prejudice 47

deception techniques 32, 34
defensive positions **28**, **29**, 30–31, **32**
    Buna **79**, **81**
    coastal **77**
    Gifu **88**
    Gona **28**, **32**
    strongpoint, South Giruwa ("Perimeter Q") **29**
"detachments" 12, 89
divisions
    1st Guards 6
    2d "Sendai" 10, 13, 14, 60, 61, 62, 63, 64
    3d 44
    3d Guards 19
    4th 14
    5th 11, 14, 44, 80
    6th 11, 14, 43, 65, 67, 70, 72
    13th and 16th 14
    17th 11, 14, 72
    18th and 19th 14
    20th 11, 14, 82, 83, 85, 86, 87
    21st 14
    29th **33**
    30th 6, 7, 14
    31st 6–7, 14
    33d 14
    35th 44, 67
    36th 44
    37th 67
    38th 10, 14, 60, 61, 63, 64
    41st 11, 14, 82, 83, 86, 87
    42d 6, 7
    43d 6, 7, 67
    46th 6, 7, 44
    47th 6, 7
    48th 44
    51st 11, 14, 64, 80, 81, 83, 84, 86
    55th and 56th 14
    58th–60th 6
    61st 6, 7
    62d 6–7

63d–65th 7
68th–71st 6
116th 14
Guards 6, 14, 18–19
Southeast area 15
doctrine 27–32, 34
Driniumor River **33**, 86
"Duty" companies 12

Eastern Solomons, Battle of the 56
Edson's Ridge, Battle of 54, 56, 58
evacuation operations **89**, 89
expansion, 1942–43 6–7

Fiji 10
flying brigades/companies/regiments 25

Gona, Papua 49
    see also Buna-Gona, Eastern New Guinea
Guadalcanal 14, 21, 27, 28, 29–30, 34, 38, 39, 48, 49, **50**, 50–52, 54, 56–58, 60–65
    evacuation, Japanese **89**, 89
    Gifu, Japanese fighting positions **88**
    Henderson Field 39, **54**, 54, **55**, 61, 63
    IJN ice plant **53**
    Matanikau River **57**, **59**, 61, 62
    Naval Battle of 64
    US Marines logistics trail **60**
Guadalcanal/Tulagi defense force 51
Guard Force, 82d 80
Guards Brigades, 1st and 2d 19
Guards divisions 6, 14, 18–19

Haruyoshi Seikichi, LtGen see Hyakutake, LtGen Seikichi
Horii Tomitaro, MajGen 72, 76, 77
horse transport **7**
Hyakutake Seikichi, LtGen 42, 70

Ichiki Detachment 54, 56, 61
Imamura Hitoshi, LtGen **43**
Imperial General Headquarters (IGHQ) 6, 9, 22, 43, 48, 49, 51, 52, 61, 64, 69, 79, 82, 84
independent mixed brigades 18
    1st 6
    21st 11, 18
    23d 7
    25th–34th 7
    China, 1942: 18
Infantry
    23d 70, 72
    41st 77
    66th 83
    124th 56, 57, 58, 64
    144th 49
        see also South Seas Detachment
    170th 77, 79
    228th 64

95